MASKS OF MYSTERY

ANCIENT CHINESE BRONZES FROM SANXINGDUI

假面之謎：三星堆出土中國古代青銅器

Liu Yang

Edmund Capon

ART GALLERY NSW

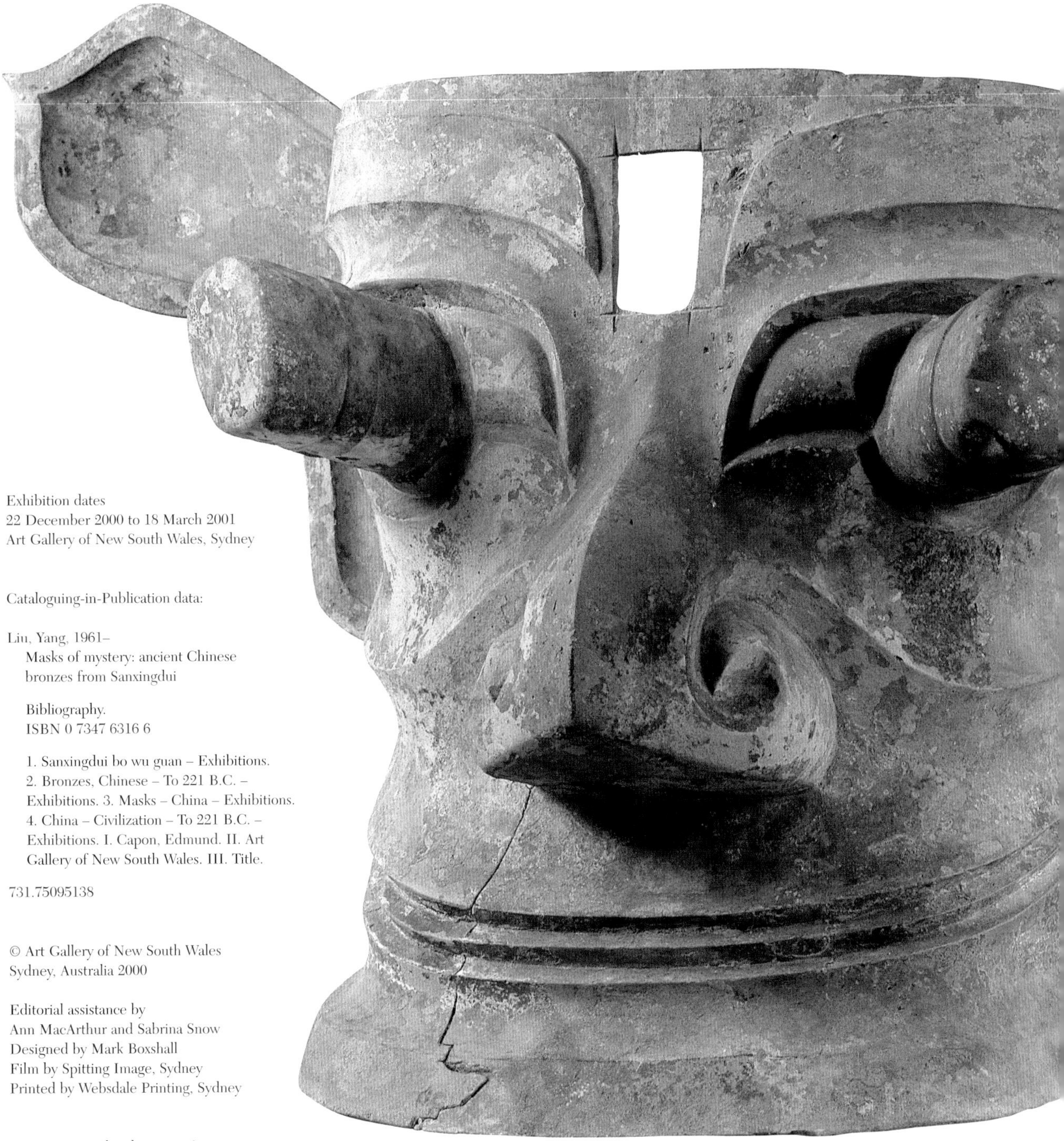

Exhibition dates
22 December 2000 to 18 March 2001
Art Gallery of New South Wales, Sydney

Cataloguing-in-Publication data:

Liu, Yang, 1961–
Masks of mystery: ancient Chinese bronzes from Sanxingdui

Bibliography.
ISBN 0 7347 6316 6

1. Sanxingdui bo wu guan – Exhibitions. 2. Bronzes, Chinese – To 221 B.C. – Exhibitions. 3. Masks – China – Exhibitions. 4. China – Civilization – To 221 B.C. – Exhibitions. I. Capon, Edmund. II. Art Gallery of New South Wales. III. Title.

731.75095138

Editorial assistance by
Ann MacArthur and Sabrina Snow
Designed by Mark Boxshall
Film by Spitting Image, Sydney
Printed by Websdale Printing, Sydney

Cover: Human head, cat. no. 1
Pages 1, 2, 111 and 112: Details of standing figure, cat. no. 5
This page: Zoomorphic human mask with protruding pupils, cat. no. 15
Page 10: The Sanxingdui site
Page 22: The excavation of Pit II at Sanxingdui
Page 47: View of Sanxingdui Pit II
Back cover: Side view of human head with a head gear, cat. no. 9

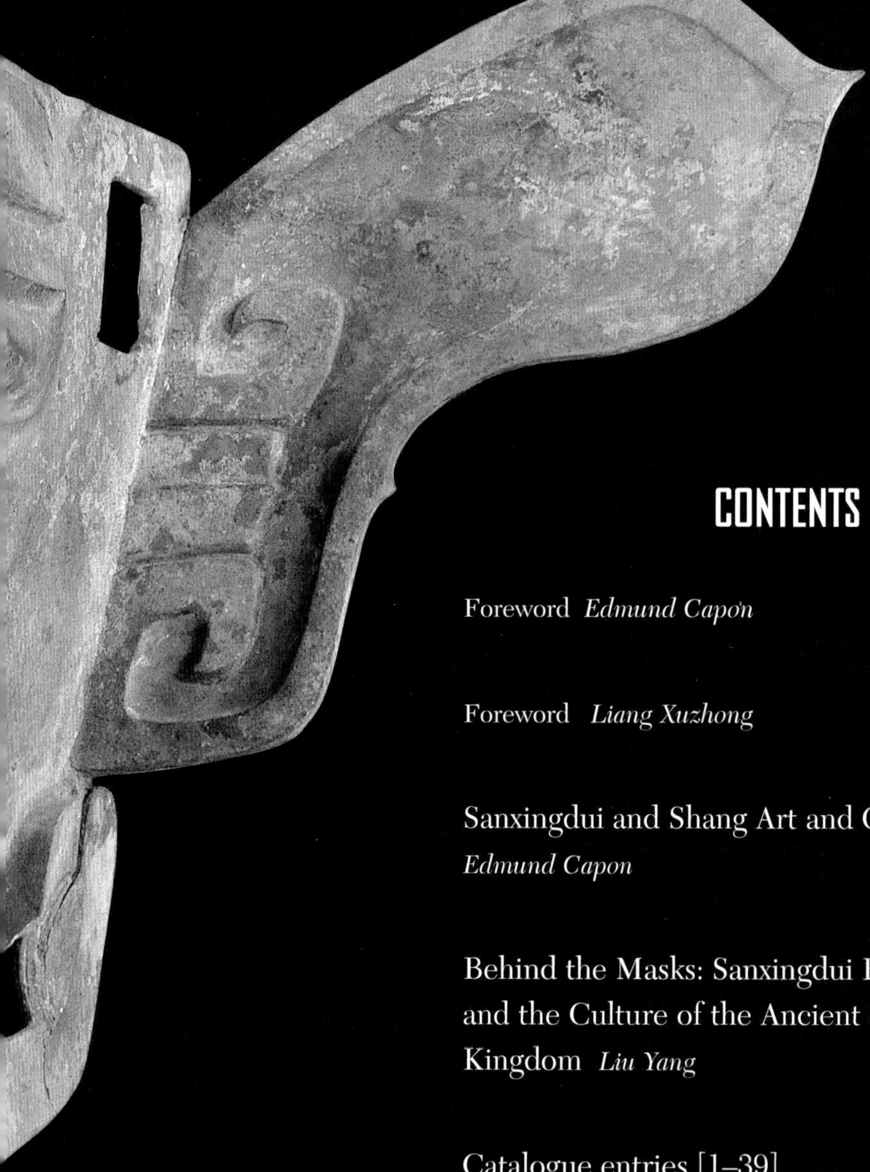

CONTENTS

FOREWORD

The last century has seen a succession of remarkable discoveries that brought to life the extraordinary achievements and imaginations of the peoples of early China. As the century dawned the adventurer-archaeologists, most notably Paul Pelliot, Albert von Le Coq and Sir Aurel Stein, were about their controversial business of rediscovering the Chinese Central Asian cultures that had lain hidden for centuries beneath the sands and which had flourished in the first millenium of our era when the fabled Silk Roads were at their height. The stunning treasures of the Thousand Buddha cave at Dunhuang, and other Buddhist sites, irresistibly stirred Western imaginations. Two decades later the discovery of the late Shang capital at Anyang confirmed the extraordinary sophistication and technical accomplishment of China's early bronze culture and brought forth the evidence, on inscribed oracle bones, for the beginnings of China's written language.

Following the establishment of the People's Republic in 1949 the relative anarchy and opportunism that had characterised the exploration of China's archaeological history was brought under control, but the pace of revelation did not slacken. In the outer environs of the ancient capital of Xian the landmark site of the neolithic Yangshao culture and its classic painted pottery, at the village of Banpo, was discovered in the 1950s. In 1968 soldiers were surprised when blasting a cliff-face near Mancheng in Hebei province to find a hollowed-out cavern where archaeologists found the first of the legendary jade burial suits dating from the Western Han dynasty of 2000 years ago; and in 1974, perhaps the most dramatic of all, was the discovery of the buried life-size pottery army of China's first emperor, Qin Shihuang. Most recently, in 1986, was the epic discovery of the amazing and drama-charged bronze masks dating from the Shang dynasty at Sanxingdui in the southwestern province of Sichuan. This exhibition is selected entirely from the objects recovered from the Sanxingdui excavations and focuses on the centrepieces of those finds, the bronze masks.

The Gallery is delighted to work with our colleagues in the Sanxingdui Museum and Sichuan Province to bring an exhibition of such rare and unique treasures to Sydney. Our special thanks to all those colleagues in China and most especially to Mr Liang Xuzhong, Director of the Sichuan Provincial Administration for Culture.

To our principal sponsor, Tower, we express our gratitude for their ready engagement with our important Asian programmes and this exhibition in particular; and to Cody Outdoors and the Landmark Parkroyal, our suppporting sponsors, we express our thanks.

Edmund Capon,
Director, Art Gallery of New South Wales

前 言

過去的一個世紀對中國考古來説，是碩果累累的一段時期。這些考古發掘活動，向世人展示了古代中國人民驚人的成就和想像力。當上個世紀進入黎明之際，一批探險家和考古學家如伯希和，勒・考克和斯坦因，正在上路，開始他們那頗具爭議的中國中亞文化的考古發掘。在那儿，深埋於黄沙底下達幾個世紀的古代文化曾於公元一世紀之際，當絲綢之路美名遠揚的時候，盛極一時；在那儿，敦煌千佛洞以及另外一些佛教遺址中的古代珍寶，激發了多少西方人的想象。二十多年後，安陽殷墟的發掘，肯定了中國早期青銅文化已達到了驚人的高度。此外，在那兒出土的甲骨文，進一步爲中國書寫文字的開端提供了活生生的證據。

隨著一九四九年中華人民共和國的建立，以往考古歷史上相對的無政府主義和機會主義現象得到了控制，但是考古活動並沒有停滯。五十年代在古都西安郊外半坡發現了新石器時代仰韶文化遺址，以及具有代表性彩陶。一九六八年，在河北滿城，解放軍士兵於山崖邊施工時，出乎意外地暴露出依山而鑿的洞穴；在那儿，考古工作者發現了第一件製作於兩千多年前西漢時代的傳奇般的玉衣。隨後，一九七四年在陝西臨潼出土了中國考古史上最富有戲劇性的的秦始皇兵馬俑。接著，在一九八六年，於西南省份四川的廣漢三星堆，史無前例地出土了商代古蜀青銅器。這個展覽中的展品，正是來自三星堆的發掘，其中心是青銅面具。

本館很高興能與四川的同行合作，在悉尼舉辦這樣一個難得的展覽。我們要特別感謝四川省文化廳副廳長梁旭仲給予我們的幫助；感謝這個展覽的主要贊助單位，Tower 保險公司；以及 Cody Outdoors, Landmark Parkroyal 等單位的大力支持。

新南威爾士藝術博物館 館長　艾德蒙・卡彭

前 言

值此中國四川三星堆出土文物在澳大利亞隆重展出之際，我對此表示熱烈的祝賀，并向爲此展覽作出了巨大努力的澳大利亞新南威爾士藝術博物館多年來對我們工作予以大力支持和理解表示深切的謝意。

三星堆古蜀國遺址位于四川省成都市北郊四十公里的廣漢市三星堆村，早在本世紀二十年代就發現大量玉石器而聞名于世。一九八六年四川省文物考古研究所在三星堆兩個祭祀坑發掘出了大批青銅器、金器具、玉石器、陶器、海貝和象牙等文物，成爲二十世紀中國考古重大發現之一。一九九八年春天，在三星堆遺址又出土了與長江下游良渚文化同時期的精美無比的玉器。三星堆文物的出土，將古蜀國的歷史向前推進了二千年到三千年，充分展示了古代成都平原燦爛的歷史文化，它不僅爲考古，歷史，青銅器鑄造工藝等等學科的研究增添了新的內容，也充分證明古蜀國是長江上遊古代文明的中心，早在三、四千年前就具有了同殷商中原文化相媲美的高度發達的文明形態，中華文明的起源是多元化的。三星堆文化與中原文化一樣都是中華民族文化寶庫中璀燦的明珠。

此次展示的三星堆文物都具有極高的歷史價值和藝術價值，展現三星堆古蜀國豐富多彩的社會風貌和光輝燦爛的歷史文化，從而爲人們了解，研究中華文明的起源提供了豐富而具體的實物資料。

文物是全人類的共同財富，也是世界各國人民相互了解，增進友誼與合作的橋樑。我深信，通過此展覽，澳大利亞人民將更進一步了解四川、了解中國，四川與澳大利亞的友誼與合作將與日俱增。

預祝三星堆文物展取得圓滿成功。

中華人民共和國四川省文物管理局 局長
梁旭仲

FOREWORD

On this memorable occasion marking the exhibition in Australia of archaeological relics discovered at Sanxingdui in Sichuan. I offer my warmest congratulations, and deepest thanks, to the Art Gallery of New South Wales for mounting this exhibition, and for the hard work they have spent in their cooperative effort with us to organise and realise this show.

The Sanxingdui site is located at Sanxingdui village in Guanghan County, 40 kilometres north of the city of Chengdu, in Sichuan province. The area became famous early in the twentieth century for discoveries of vast quantities of jade and stone artefacts. In 1986 an excavation carried out by the Sichuan Provincial Institute of Archaeology unearthed, from two sacrificial pits at the Sanxingdui site, large quantities of relics such as bronzes, gold implements, jades, pottery, cowrie shell and elephant tusks. This discovery was to constitute the major archaeological find in 20th century China. In the spring of 1998, the excavations at Sanxingdui also disclosed some unique jade pieces of exquisite quality which are contemporary with the Liangzhu culture on the lower Yangzi. The archaeological finds advanced the known history of the ancient Shu by two to three thousand years and brought to light the rich cultural history of the Chengdu plain. Not only did the discovery provide new information on archaeology and history adding new substance to scientific knowledge of such aspects as bronze casting techniques, but it also irrefutably proved that the ancient Shu Kingdom was the centre of civilisation on the upper Yangzi River in antiquity. About three to four thousand years ago a culture was already established here civilised enough to rival that which developed in the metropolitan Shang area.

The exhibition of artefacts from Sanxingdui has a very high artistic and cultural value. It will reveal the richness of the social customs and dazzling cultural background of the Shu kingdom, providing a wealth of factual evidence, which can enable people to understand the origins of Chinese civilisation.

Archaeological artefacts are a resource to be shared by all mankind, one that can act as a bridge people of all nations, promoting understanding, friendship and cooperation. I strongly believe that this exhibition will mark a forward step in the growth of understanding between Australia and Sichuan and China generally, enabling the cooperation and friendship between us to grow stronger with each day. I wish the exhibition every success.

Liang Xuzhong,
Head of the Sichuan Provincial Administration for Cultural Relics,
People's Republic of China

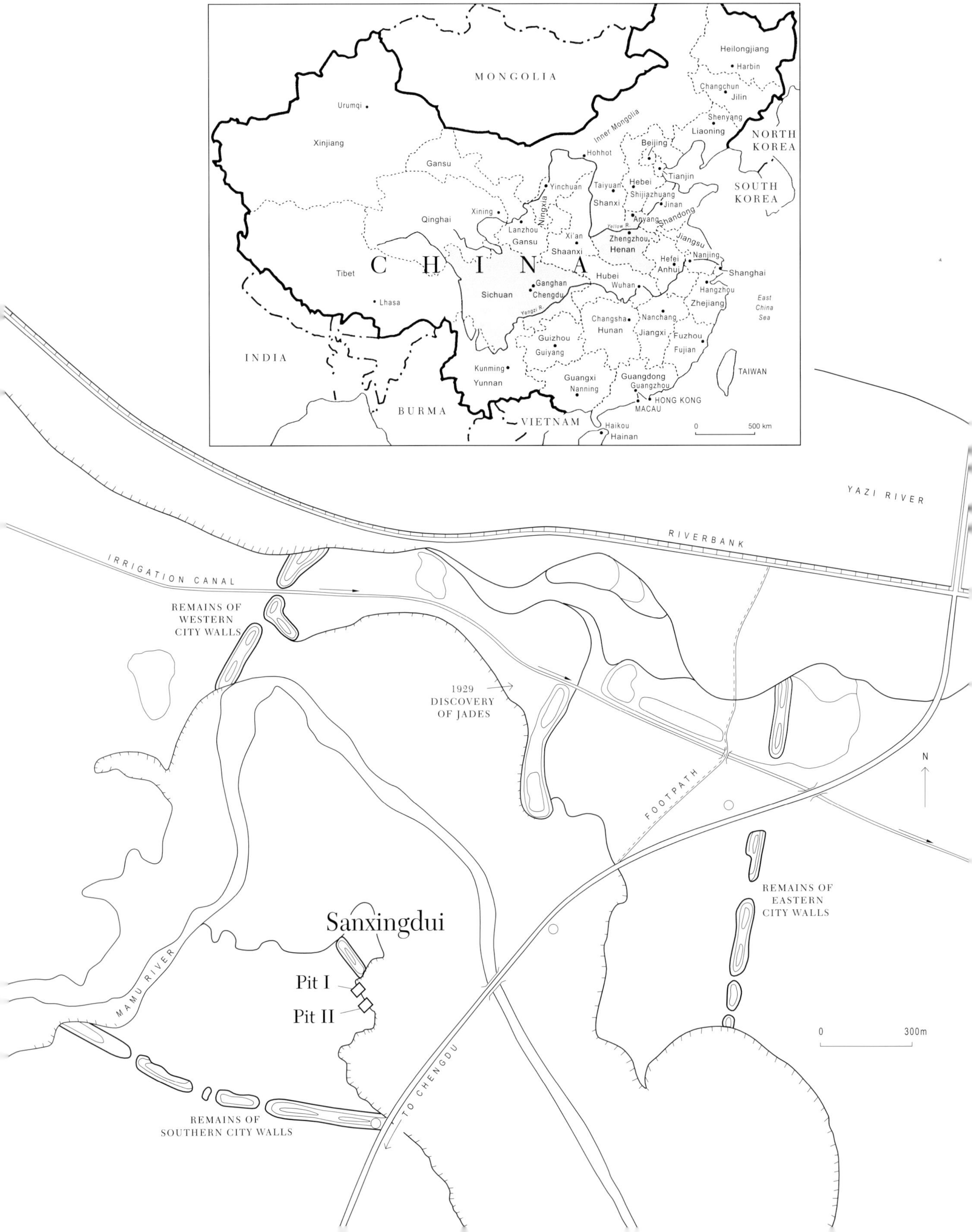
MONGOLIA
Heilongjiang
Harbin
Changchun
Jilin
Urumqi
Xinjiang
Inner Mongolia
Shenyang
Liaoning
NORTH KOREA
Beijing
Hohhot
Gansu
Tianjin
Yinchuan
Taiyuan
Hebei
Shijiazhuang
SOUTH KOREA
Ningxia
Shanxi
Jinan
Xining
Anyang
Shandong
Qinghai
Lanzhou
Yellow R.
Gansu
Xi'an
Zhengzhou
Jiangsu
Shaanxi
Henan
Nanjing
Hefei
Anhui
Shanghai
Tibet
C H I N A
Hubei
Wuhan
Ganghan
Hangzhou
Sichuan
Chengdu
East China Sea
Lhasa
Yangzi R.
Changsha
Nanchang
Zhejiang
Hunan
Jiangxi
Fuzhou
Guizhou
Fujian
Guiyang
INDIA
Kunming
TAIWAN
Yunnan
Guangxi
Guangdong
Guangzhou
Nanning
HONG KONG
MACAU
BURMA
VIETNAM
Haikou
Hainan
0
500 km
YAZI RIVER
RIVERBANK
IRRIGATION CANAL
REMAINS OF WESTERN CITY WALLS
1929 DISCOVERY OF JADES
N
FOOTPATH
REMAINS OF EASTERN CITY WALLS
Sanxingdui
Pit I
Pit II
MAMU RIVER
0
300m
TO CHENGDU
REMAINS OF SOUTHERN CITY WALLS

SANXINGDUI AND SHANG ART AND CULTURE

EDMUND CAPON

The image of China's first great and assuredly identified dynasty, the Shang (c. 1600–1100 BCE), is indelibly and powerfully determined in the achievements of its bronze culture. It is a unique image steeped in the ritual and symbolism of ancient rites and ceremonies, and immortalised in bronze vessels and accoutrements of extraordinary technical accomplishment and aesthetic sophistication.

The range of Shang dynasty ritual bronze vessels, from tripod drinking cups to food containers and exotic wine vessels, is richly diverse in form but fully homogenous in spirit. Their unusual, often eccentric, forms and shapes would seem to deny any sense of functional evolution, although certain earlier Neolithic period ceramic types do herald selected bronze counterparts. Similarly their mysterious ornament echoes the ancient rites, ceremonies and sacrifices that they serviced. They are vessels that truly convey the power and arcane authority of the rituals, beliefs and values that defined a culture of the remote past.

There has, understandably, been much debate about the relatively sudden appearance of such a technically advanced and conceptually sophisticated bronze culture with few apparent precedents, however, certain late Neolithic pottery types may clearly be identified as prototypes. The classic Neolithic pottery-based cultures of Yangshao in the Yellow River valley and Longshan in Shandong province have both produced pottery vessels that preface bronze vessel types: for example, the tripod *jue* wine vessel and the *gu* beaker.[1] Similarly in the painted decoration on certain red pottery vessels from the landmark Yangshao Neolithic site at Banpo near Xian in Shaanxi province and other related sites are designs that, in their stylisation and manipulation into an elongated band form of a geometric mask-like face, may be seen as a primitive

Figure 1.
Painted pottery design from the Yangshao neolithic culture: Banpo, Xian, Shaanxi province; circa 3500 BCE; *taotie* mask design from a ritual bronze *ding* vessel of the early Shang period c. 14–12th century BCE (Shanghai Museum).

precursor to the ubiquitous *taotie* monster mask of Bronze Age China (see fig. 1). So ubiquitous is that motif that it appears in the bronzes recovered from Sanxingdui.

Whilst it is certainly beyond dispute that it is bronzes: vessels, fittings, fixtures and weapons, which are the indelible hallmark of the Shang and indeed of China's Bronze Age cultures, the level of material cultural achievement may also be measured in parallel advances in ceramic technology, in the notion of a written language and in the art of fashioning jades. Such tangible achievements are the material manifestations of concepts and ideas that demonstrate values and aspirations of a society far advanced on those of the subsistence levels of its Neolithic predecessor. It is this factor of cultural and social structure, and the technological advances, which distinguishes China's Bronze Age from its Neolithic predecessor. The Neolithic was essentially a village-based agrarian society identified by its pottery culture, and the Shang was a city-state with the concept of a centralised government and a cultural authority expressed in its bronze industry.

The heart of Shang culture lay in the Yellow River valley in present-day Henan province and the eastern regions of neighbouring Shaanxi province. From excavations at the principal Shang dynasty sites at Erlitou, Zhengzhou and the dynasty's renowned and final capital, Anyang, all in Henan province, have been recovered an astonishing panorama of ritual bronze vessels, as well as jade carvings, more rudimentary ceramics and, particularly at Anyang, the highly significant oracle bones with their interpretative inscriptions that are evidently the origins of the Chinese written language. Dedicatory inscriptions on bronze vessels, bearing clan or personal names and more rarely indicating the event relating to the ceremony or sacrifice for which the vessel was made, further illustrate the early development of the Chinese language.

From these heartlands the modest diaspora of Shang culture, conveyed most powerfully in bronze vessels, spread westwards to Shaanxi, northwards to Hebei and Shanxi, eastwards to Shandong, and southwards to the Yangzi valley and the provinces of Anhui, Hunan and Jiangxi. The overriding influence of mainstream Shang culture is manifest in the bronze cultures of these more peripheral regions, which are indisputably related to their metropolitan Yellow River valley counterparts, but conditioned by local or provincial dialects in terms of both form and decoration. Certain vessel types, so strongly identified with the central yellow River culture, for example the tripod *jue* and the beaker-like *gu*, are seldom if ever encountered in the repertoire of provincial bronze vessel types. Generally the range of vessel types and the sophistication of the intricate designs are greater on bronzes from those traditional heartlands. The range of ritual wine and food vessels from the central Henan sites number at least twenty, whilst from the periphery of the empire, in for example the provinces of Hunan, Anhui and Jiangxi, the range is a more modest five or six different vessel types. It is similarly true that the further removed from the heartlands the greater the tendency for deviations from the tense and disciplined decorative and symbolic designs so characteristic of mature Shang dynasty bronzes. The tension of restraint is released in a more gregarious decorative aesthetic with a preference for moments of flourish, higher relief décor and structural features such as flanges, all of which contrast with the quiet but complex surface patterns of the high Shang style. And yet such bronzes, from the further corners of the Shang sphere of influence, are clearly within the mainstream cultural and artistic style of the Shang. The central motif of Shang bronze décor, the almost ubiquitous *taotie* monster mask, still forms the basis of symbolic design on all these provincial types and variations of bronze vessels.

One province that rarely appears in this view of Shang dynasty sites is Sichuan, which makes the Sanxingdui finds all the more remarkable. Prior to the discovery in 1986 of the two pits at Sanxingdui there had been very little material evidence for the existence of a related Shang culture in the region. As early as the 1930s archaeologists had identified the locality as a potentially rich archaeological source and in the early 1980s excavations had revealed city walls built in the familiar Shang method of layers of pounded earth. In the course of preliminary excavations a chronology from the late second millennium BCE, corresponding to late Neolithic times, to the early Western Zhou period of the 10th century BCE, was established. These excavations, however, revealed only the existence of a settlement and it was not until 1986 and the incidental discovery of the sacrificial pits and their contents of these remarkable and unique works of art that the reality of a mature Shang society in Sichuan could be firmly established. Furthermore, these finds declare a Shang society of great distinction and individuality in having clear aesthetic and ideological associations with the metropolitan Yellow River culture, but one uniquely conditioned with a radical local imagination. The powerful, mesmerising and strangely ominous masks from Sanxingdui are wholly unlike anything from the panorama of contemporary Shang art.

The association of the Sanxingdui finds with mainstream Shang art is nonetheless, determined in other bronzes and jades recovered from the site, for along with those amazing masks, were found a small range of ritual vessels, particularly the *zun* and *lei* types, and carved jades, all of which correspond with types from Shang sites across the country. Whilst the range of vessel types is limited, what is of significance is that in both form and decoration they are firmly within the Shang aesthetic and in their casting and manufacture display similar high levels of technical accomplishment. It may also be assumed that the Sanxingdui vessels performed the same kind of ritual and ceremonial functions as those from other sites in that they are of similar, if not identical, shape and bear ornament of similar inspiration and symbolic value. The fundamental motif of

Shang bronzes, the *taotie* mask, appears in its most sophisticated form on, for example, a number of *zun* vessels recovered from Pit II at Sanxingdui and is, at first glance, virtually indistinguishable from similar designs on vessels from the capital at Anyang. Close inspection does reveal subtle differences in detail and emphasis that may be characterised as a contrast of the sense of flourish in the regional designs with the tense formality of the classic metropolitan Shang style. For example, on the bronze *zun* vessel from Pit II (fig. 2) the *taotie* masks that are the basic elements of the designs of the panels around the body and the footrim are enhanced with 'quill'-like motifs, which invoke a slight sense of individuality into the interpretation and thereby offer some contrast to the sublime formality of the classic Anyang style: one that is well illustrated on a bronze rectangular *ding* vessel in this Gallery's collection (fig. 3).

Such individuality is, however, familiar in other regional interpretations, and that same 'quill'-like motif may also be identified on other bronze ritual vessels from the peripheral regions of the Shang empire: a bronze *hu* vase excavated in 1989 in Jiangxi province in the south,[2] and a *pou* vessel from northerly Hebei province,[3] and in yet another variant form on a splendid *zun* vase that was

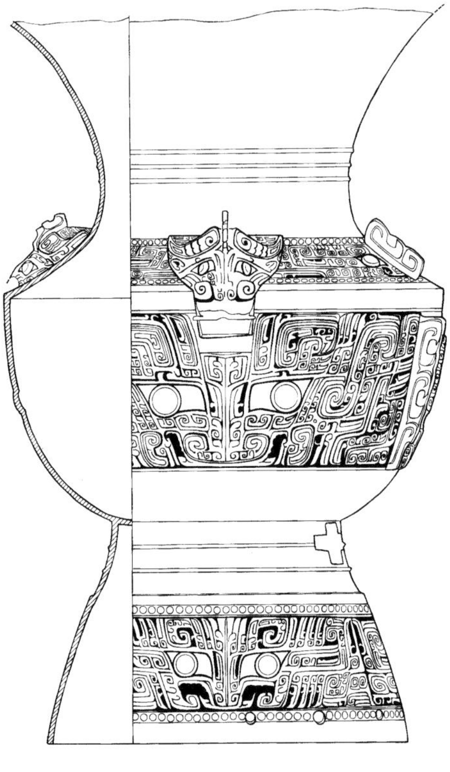

Figure 2. Drawing of a vessel from Sanxingdui Pit II (K2(2): 109): on the lower decorative band are the 'quill'-like motifs ornamenting the *taotie* mask.

Figure 3. Detail of the *taotie* mask on a rectangular bronze ritual vessel *ding*; Shang dynasty. Art Gallery of New South Wales.

Figure 4. Bronze ritual vessel *zun*: height 47 cm. Shang dynasty, c. 13th–12th century BCE, excavated at Funan, Anhui province. Museum of Chinese History, Biejing.

Figure 5. Bronze ritual vessel *zun*: height 43.3 cm (K1: 158,258) Shang dynasty.

Figure 6. Bronze ritual vessel *zun*: height 56.5 cm (K2(2): 151) Shang dynasty; from Sanxingdui Pit II.

excavated in Anhui province in 1957 and was included in 'The Chinese Exhibition' of recent archaeological discoveries of China held in Australia in 1977 (fig. 4).[4] Another association of these peripheral Shang styles is illustrated in the distinctive design on another *zun* vessel from Pit I at Sanxingdui (fig. 5) which comprises a pair of elongated feline bodies meeting with a common head. A similar design is to be found on a *zun* vessel excavated in 1957 at Funan in Anhui (the site from which the *zun* vessel referred to above (fig. 4) was recovered)[5] demonstrating an apparently strong relationship between these regional centres of Shang culture even though these two sites, Sanxingdui in Sichuan and Funan in Anhui, are separated by some 1500 kilometres. A similar design appears in a very specific and serpentine way on a rectangular bronze *ding* vessel, datable to the very end of the Shang dynasty, and now in the Freer Gallery of Art in Washington.[6]

There are also slight but significant variations in the shapes of similar vessel types. The most characteristic of the Sanxingdui ritual vessels is the *zun*, a vase-like vessel with a footrim, prominent shoulder and flaring mouth; usually round although square types are also known and include the fragments of a single vessel from Pit II at Sanxingdui. However, like the decorative system, local variations are distinctive and distinguish these regional types from their metropolitan counterparts; for example, a number of these vessels from Sanxingdui have relatively high and slightly curved footrims (fig. 6) that are in some contrast to the more common splayed foot or lower footrim characteristic to *zun* vessels from the Yellow River valley. Once again though the Sanxingdui variations in form find parallels in *zun* vessels recovered from other regional Shang sites.[7] Pit II at Sanxingdui contained the greatest number of ritual bronze vessels, and in addition to the eight *zun* vessel types found, were a number of the less usual *lei* vessel which again in both form and decoration has distinctive variations. In shape

Figure 7. Bronze ritual vessel *lei*: height 35.4 cm; Shang dynasty; from Sanxingdui Pit II (K2(2): 88).

the *lei* is a sturdier and stouter version of the *zun* with a broader body, no flaring mouth and often fitted with a lid (fig. 7). Typical types from the north are of square cross-section and gradually expanding girth from the base up, whereas those from Sanxingdui are more closely modelled on the *zun* with distinctive footrim and body.

Such features clearly give the Sichuan bronze ritual vessels from Sanxingdui their distinctive and slightly independent flavour. They do, however, very firmly demonstrate their cultural, artistic and hierarchical allegiance to the Shang sphere of influence. However distinctive, unusual and at times even eccentric these bronze ritual vessels from Sanxingdui may be, they indisputably belong to Shang dynasty China. Having established their profound relationship with Shang art and culture it is pertinent to consider, in that context, the extraordinary uniqueness of the Sanxingdui finds. Central to these are, of course, the remarkable bronze masks, heads and the life-size figure, but in addition to these spectacular objects there are others: bronze fittings, bird and animal subjects, of equal distinction. These objects similarly fall within the Shang sphere of artistic imagination and technical accomplishment and yet express an undeniable local individuality. In terms of style and interpretation a number of modestly scaled bird and human head and figure finials (see cat. nos 24, 25, 26) similarly express that quality of local individuality and are unlike anything else from Shang China.

Spectacularly different is the imposing bird head of dramatic profile and powerful symbolic value (cat. no. 23). And yet, distinctive and unique though it is, aesthetically it too is consistent with the Shang tradition. The bold eye with its strongly stylised definition is a clear echo of the manner in which the horns and features of the *taotie* mask is defined on a whole range of bronze vessels; and the hooked flange on the neck of the bird is paralleled by flanges on a number of specific types, especially the rectangular *ding* and *fangyi* vessel types.

Above all in its authoritative presence this object, inspired by reality but transformed into an object of almost deified dimensions, presides with a similar symbolic power to that possessed by the most powerful of ritual vessels and the masks themselves. Whilst there is no disputing the uniqueness of this object, the bird as a motif in Shang art, is familiar to bronze vessels from both the Yellow River heartlands and from the outer regions of the empire. A bronze *yu*, a lidded container, excavated in 1971 in Hunan province and a similar vessel discovered in Henan province, firmly within the heartlands of Shang dynasty China, are both ornamented with exotic birds with prominent 'hooked' beaks in the spirit of, but certainly not identical to, the massive Sanxingdui example.[8] Generally the bird motif appears in Shang art and even more so in the bronzes of the succeeding Western Zhou period, more as a component of the design than as an independent object which, once again, makes this impressive bird head all the more unexpected within the artistic traditions of the Shang dynasty.

In considering other motifs and designs common to the repertoire of bronze decoration, the Sanxingdui finds generally conform to Shang principles. The dominant features of Shang dynasty bronze ritual vessel ornament are the *taotie* mask; a formalised cicada motif that is often inscribed within a geometric pattern of either horizontal or vertical format; a mythical beast known as a *kui* dragon; various bovine and feline animal masks; the occasional bird motif and variations of a spiral, or *leiwen*, background pattern.

The ritual bronze vessels from Sanxingdui in general adhere to the spirit of the strongly symbolic ornamental style of Shang period art. The *taotie* mask is, as already noted, the fundamental decorative feature, and usually set against a spiral pattern background that is equally synonomous with the Shang style. The *kui* dragon motif appears in an even more evolved manner at Sanxingdui, often partially incorporated into the horns of the *taotie* mask: for example on the *zun* vessel (fig. 8). Animal, particularly bovine, heads appear frequently on the Sanxingdui material and, more distinctively, unexpected appendages such as small bird motifs (fig. 9). However, such distinctions are essentially differences of detail, for within the tradition of bronze ritual vessels the Sanxingdui examples are wholly identified with the Shang style.

Figure 8. Rubbing from the design on a ritual bronze *zun* illustrating incorporation of the *kui* dragon motif into the *taotie* mask design; from Sanxingdui Pit II (K2(2): 127).

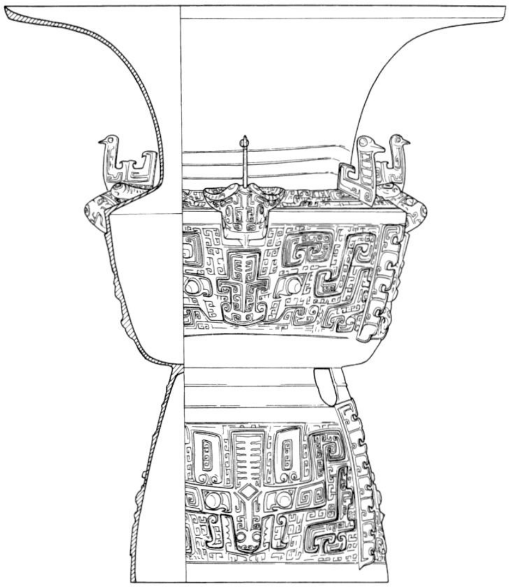

Figure 9. Drawing of bronze ritual vessel *zun* showing the bird motif on the shoulder of the vessel; from Sanxingdui Pit II (K2(2): 146).

This is more than can be said for the mysterious bronze fittings in the form of a five-spoke wheel and others which are large diamond-shaped objects, neither of which are remotely like anything else in the whole repertoire of bronze objects, fittings and vessels of the Shang dynasty (cat. nos 28 and 29). Speculation and uncertainty surrounds the role of the circular objects, which may be functional as a base for a ceremonial object for example, or may be symbolic as an emblem of, perhaps, the sun. The diamond-shaped objects appear to resemble eyes, or eye-coverings, to perhaps another image of immense scale. These most enigmatic and seemingly functional objects challenge our imaginations as to their role, just as they deny any sense of association with the principal traditions of Shang bronze art.

Of great significance is the extent to which mainstream Shang stylistic and decorative instincts and motifs appear in the more unusual and individualistic works from Sanxingdui, for this re-affirms that relationship between the Sichuan and Yellow river cultures. The most remarkable figure of all, the virtually life-size priest or shaman, quite unique in early Chinese art (cat. no. 5), is nonetheless ornamented with motifs and designs that are fully within the Shang aesthetic, in spirit if not in detail. In certain details, particularly the rectangular band designs on the crown or headpiece which are similar to those on another head in the exhibition (cat. no. 6), it prefaces the bolder design aesthetic of later Western Zhou bronzes. The austerity and authority of the figure itself is mysteriously well served by the symbolic detail of its surface ornament which is dominated by variant forms of the *taotie* mask and other dragon-like motifs and composite decorative devices. Around the hem are further designs that echo the *taotie* mask, beneath which are blade-shaped motifs which relate to the so-called 'hanging blade' design, incorporating a stylised cicada motif, familiar to so many Shang ritual vessels including a circular bronze *ding* in this Gallery's collection.[9] Even the robust architectonic dimensions and designs of the pedestal, on which this most unique of objects – the bronze figure – stands, echo the Shang decorative aesthetic.

Inevitably the powerfully mysterious and strangely futuristic heads and masks are the hallmark objects of the Sanxingdui finds. The representation of the human figure and the human face in mainstream Shang art is rare and largely confined to a small number of ritual vessels with mask-like faces as a part of their ornament and a similarly small number of carved jade images. The revelation of the Sanxingdui finds thus adds a dramatic and unexpected new dimension to the established image of Shang art. Among the very few human images known in Shang bronzes are: a rectangular *ding* vessel with human faces on each of its four sides that was excavated in 1959 in Hunan province and included in 'The Chinese Exhibition' in Australia in 1977,[10] and the similar gently realistic human face on the lid of a *he*, kettle, vessel in the Freer Gallery of Art in Washington.[11] In both of these examples, and others such as the two *yu* (lidded bucket) vessels in the form of monsters devouring a human figure, one in the Musée Cernuschi in Paris and the other in the Sumitomo Collection in Kyoto,[12] the human figure not only plays a subsidiary role but also one that tends to be more 'human' than ritualistically symbolic like the Sanxingdui heads and masks.

The whole notion of realism, and indeed the human figure, in Shang art is fundamentally alien to its aesthetic driven by the needs of symbolism in the service of ritual, sacrifice and ceremony. Certain bronze vessels were made in the form of birds and animals, examples of which include *zun* vessels in the shape of owls (an example is in the V & A Museum in London)[13] and elephants (in the Avery Brundage collection in the Asian Art Museum of San Francisco)[14] with considerable levels of fidelity to the real appearance of the subject, but even in such cases their symbolic and ritualistic character is persuasive and undeniable.

On other vessels vaguely recognisable forms, animal, bovine and feline in nature and inspiration, regularly appear but their realism is subverted by a ritualistic and symbolic spirit.

Closest in symbolic power and presence to the Sanxingdui human-inspired masks and heads is, probably, an unusual double-faced finial that was excavated in 1989 from a tomb in Xingan county in the southern province of Jiangxi, like Sanxingdui well-distanced from the heartlands of the Shang empire.[15] This somewhat frightening object, with its two antennae, has circular holes for eyes, which may have once held tubular protrusions like the large Sanxingdui masks. However, in many respects this strange object with its *taotie*-like mouth is even further removed from human reality than the Sanxingdui heads and masks. It is more in its symbolic value that it equates to the Sichuan heads. A similar rudimentary sense of realism is to be seen in the few carved jades of human and animal subjects dating from the Shang dynasty, but none from Sanxingdui where the only jade objects found have been ritualistc sceptres, daggers, and other purely symbolic items. The human and animal jade carvings are inevitably small in scale and some of the most interesting and convincing known examples are recent discoveries. In 1976 the tomb of Fu Hao was discovered: she was the consort of the King Wuding who ruled towards the end of the Shang dynasty when its capital was at Anyang – the site of so many great archaeological finds. Interestingly inscriptions on oracle bones found at Anyang refer to the King Wuding having attacked the kingdom of Shu 蜀, the kingdom in the Chengdu plains of Sichuan in which Sanxingdui is situated. Although perhaps a tenuous link, it does suggest the extent of the Shang empire and the capacity of its Imperial armies to range far and wide from their bases in the Yellow River valley and thereby imply the scope of the Shang cultural sphere.

The tomb of Fu Hao revealed, in addition to the usual range of bronze vessels, a large number of jade carvings and many unexpected subjects including human figures, a coiled dragon and an endearing elephant. Although virtually miniatures, for example a plaque in the form of a standing figure is just 12.5 cm high, these objects do demonstrate a mild attempt at realism.[16] However, with their mask-like features even these attempts at realism fall far short of true imitation and retain those inevitable symbolic values inherent in Shang art. The representation of the human figure in Shang art is, therefore, exceptional. In the repertoire of bronze vessel forms and decorative schemes the human figure or face makes only rare appearances and on those rare occasions the role is naturally subservient to the ritualistic and ceremonial requirements. In such a visual culture the appearance of the dramatic Sanxingdui heads and masks is truly unexpected. These extraordinary, powerful and profoundly mysterious objects are without parallel in the history of early Chinese art. They are, however, convincing evidence of certain and accepted characteristics of the art of Bronze Age China – of an impressively high level of technological accomplishment; of a sophisticated aesthetic in its ornamental and decorative concepts; and of an impressive maturity in the notions of ritual and hierarchy that is expressed in its range of vessels.

As objects from deep antiquity the finds at Sanxingdui are astonishing in both concept and execution. We can only wonder at the circumstances and imaginations that inspired these objects and the complex rites and ceremonies that they served. Their scale, symbolic presence and echoes of another and profoundly remote world make these objects remarkable and unique, even within the annals of Shang and Bronze Age art. The uncertainty of their symbolism and role, and the circumstances of their evident and deliberate destruction prior to burial with other valuable and ritual paraphernalia, amidst a turmoil of elephant tusks and charred animal bones, only serves to heighten the mystery surrounding these stunning 3000 year-old objects.

Notes

1. Examples of both the tripod vessel and the beaker, from the Longshan neolithic culture and datable to c. 2500–2000 BCE, were included in *The Chinese Exhibition* in Australia; held in Melbourne, Sydney and Adelaide in 1977: see cat. nos 35, 36 and 40.
2. See *Zhong guo wenwu jinghua dacidian: qingtong juan*. 中國文物精華大辭典 Shanghai 1995, no. 0104, p. 30.
3. See *Zhong guo meishu quanji: no. 4 qingtong ji*. 中國美術全集，青銅器 Wen Wu Press, Beijing 1992; no. 72, p. 67.
4. The 'quill'-like motif is also seen to good effect on a *lei* ritual vessel in the Palace Museum, Beijing; see *The Great Bronze Age of China*, exhibition catalogue, Metropolitan Museum of Art, New York 1980, cat. no. 14.
5. Illustrated in *Zhong guo meishu quanji:no. 4 qingtong ji* (op. cit); no. 101, p. 92.
6. See Pope et. al. *The Freer Chinese Bronzes*, Vol. 1, Washington 1967; plate 34. Another vessel in the Freer, a *fangyi*, has a variant of this motif: see plate 36 and fig. 29 on page 203. Yet another example is on a *fang hu* vessel excavated in 1976 from a tomb near Anyang: see *Mysteries of Ancient China*, exhibition catalogue, British Museum, London 1996, cat. no. 44.
7. For example a *zun* vessel on a high footrim excavated at Huarong, Anhui province in 1967; illustrated in *Zhong guo wenwu jinghua tacidian* (op. cit); no. 0085, p. 25.
8. Both vessels are illustrated in *Zhong guo wenwu jinghua tacidian* (op. cit); no. 0126 and 0128 on pages 36 and 37 respectively; the latter is well illustrated in *The Great Bronze Age of China* (op. cit) cat. no. 25; and *China 5000 Years*, Guggenheim Museum, New York 1998, cat. no. 26.
9. See *Art Gallery of New South Wales Handbook*, 1999; p. 246.
10. See *The Chinese Exhibition* in Australia (op. cit); cat. no. 59.
11. Pope et. al *The Freer Chinese Bronzes* (op. cit); plate 39.
12. The Sumitomo example is illustrated in W. Willetts, *The Foundations of Chinese Art*, London 1965, plate 65 and W. Watson, *Ancient Chinese Bronzes*, London 1962 and 1977, plate 36a, and the Cernuschi example in V. Elisseeff, *Bronzes Archaiques Chinois*, Paris 1977; pp. 122–131.
13. Another splendid owl *zun* was found in the Shang Dynasty tomb of Fu Hao at Anyang in 1976. See *China 5000 Years* (op. cit), cat. no. 24.
14. The elephant appears more regularly as a vessel form: in addition to the Brundage example, others include one excavated in 1975 at Liling in Hunan province (see *China 5000 Years*; cat. no. 25) and a smaller model is in the Freer Gallery of Art (see *The Freer Chinese Bronzes*, no. 40).
15. See *Zhong guo wenwu qinghua dacidian* (op. cit); no. 0269; also illustrated in *The Golden Age of Chinese Archaeology*, exhibition catalogue, National Gallery of Art, Washington 1999, cat. no. 57.
16. Illustrated in *The Great Bronze Age of China* (op. cit); cat. nos 37–40.

三星堆與商代的藝術和文化

商代青銅器，盡管形式各異，但卻精神如一。它們那神秘的紋飾彷彿在向我們講述遙遠的古代的祭祀和禮儀，威權和價值。技術上如此進步，觀念上如此成熟的青銅文化，給人的感覺彷彿是橫空出世，然而，黄河流域的仰韶文化和山東的龍山文化的陶器，早已預示了青銅器的類型和紋飾。舉例來説，仰韶文化彩陶上那幾何形類似假面的紋樣，或許就是後來青銅器上饕餮紋的原型。

黄河流域的河南省，乃是當時以青銅器爲標誌的商文化的中心。從這里商文化向四方傳播開去，西到陜西，北至山西，河北，東到山東，南至長江流域的安徽，湖南和江西，強大的主流文化影響透過這些地區的青銅器反映出來。一般而言，商文化中心地區的青銅器種類繁多，設計也更成熟。離這個中心地區越遠，原本儼格遵循的象征性紋飾也出現變化。在這些地方，青銅器更偏好高浮雕的設計，附加凸出的裝飾物，這與正統的商禮器所具有的繁複卻沉靜的風格形成了強烈的對比。

比較而言，四川是一個相對獨立的地區，這使得三星堆的發現更爲不同凡響。三星堆文化，既高度獨立，又與中原文化有千絲萬縷的聯係。這點可以由祭祀坑中出土的青銅禮器，尤其是尊和罍，以及玉器來證明 - 它們在類型上很接近那些流行於河南的同樣器物，饕餮紋也同樣被使用。由于形式和裝飾風格的接近，我們還可以進一步假設，三星堆青銅禮器與中原及其它地區的同類器物具備同樣的象征內涵和禮儀功能。除了河南，三星堆藝術與非中原地區文化也有密切的聯係。一個典型例子是一號坑出土的“虎食人尊”（圖5），相似的紋飾早已在57年安徽阜南出土的尊上見到。這兩件青銅器展示了商代地域性文化中心之間的緊密聯係。三星堆最有特色的禮器是尊，寬圈足，聳肩，侈口。高圈足這個特點顯然是它不同於中原同類器物之處（圖6）。不過相似的尊反而在非中原地區有所發現。除了尊，二號坑還出土了一定數目的罍。典型的中原地區的罍常呈方形，從底座向上漸漸加寬。但三星堆的罍更象是尊的變體，口收小，器腹加大。但不論蜀地的禮器形體怎樣新穎，從根本上講，它們仍可以納入商文化的範疇之內。事實上，只有把三星堆青銅器放在與商文化藝術的聯係之中，它的獨特與不同凡響才能被更好地認識。

在三星堆所發現的器物中，那些青銅頭像，面具和立人像當然是注目的中心，但除此之外，那里還有另外一些杰出的東西，例如青銅掛飾，動物和鳥。特別不同凡響的是那件青銅鳥頭。它既富有地方特色，又同樣符合商的美學。它那風格化的眼睛的處理方式，讓人想起中原禮器的饕餮紋，它的肉冠彷彿是響應商禮器鼎和方彝上的棱脊。一般而言，三星堆青銅禮器追隨商藝術那種具有強烈象征意味的裝飾紋樣。饕餮紋依然是最基本的圖案，壓在雷紋之上；夔紋在這兒顯得更成熟；動物頭部常被用來作裝飾，比如尊肩上的小鳥。三星堆與中原青銅禮器之間的不同之處是在細節上而非整體上。最能説明三星堆與中原之間文化上的聯係的，莫過于典型的商的裝飾紋樣，出現於那些三星堆所特有的青銅器上。比如那尊眞人大小立人像，乃是迄今所知絶無僅有的作品。但即使在它的身上，我們也能見到變形的饕餮紋和蟬紋。

那些造型奇特的頭像和面具，可以當之無愧地成爲三星堆藝術的標誌性作品。它們的出現填補了商主流藝術的空白，因爲在中原地區，人像大多用作禮器上的裝飾圖案，表現風格也更寫實。其實在商藝術中，寫實的概念與那被祭祀需要所驅動的美學是格格不入的。當人物形象作爲裝飾紋樣偶爾在禮器中出現時，它自然地服從祭禮的要求。在這樣的背景中，三星堆的人像因此顯得更出人意外和無與倫比。

BEHIND THE MASKS: SANXINGDUI BRONZES AND THE CULTURE OF THE ANCIENT SHU KINGDOM

LIU YANG

1. The Discovery of the Sanxingdui Pits

Some of the most significant archaeological discoveries in China have come about by accident. On 18 July 1986, while digging for clay to make bricks at Sanxingdui in Guanghan, a county forty kilometres north of Chengdu in Sichuan province, the workers of a local brick factory came upon a collection of jades. Archaeologists were immediately called to the spot. The result of this lucky discovery was the spectacular find of Sanxingdui Pit I. On 14 August 1986, when the archaeologists had just finished with Pit I, the brickyard workers discovered, again by accident, a second pit just 30 metres from the first.

Pit I was rectangular in shape – 4.64 metres long by 3.48 metres wide and 1.64 metres deep. Altogether 420 items were unearthed amongst which were 178 bronzes, four items of gold, 129 jade artefacts, 70 works in stone, and 39 pottery objects. In addition, along with some three cubic metres of charred animal bones, there were 13 elephant tusks (identified as the *Elephas maximus*), 62 cowrie shells and a number of pieces of amber. Careful observation revealed that the objects in the pit were not disposed randomly: the jades had been dropped first into the pit, followed by the items of gold. Next were the bronze figures and vessels; then a mixed group of jades, bronze weapons, pottery, animal bones and the elephant tusks. Finally the jade of the types known as *zhang* (trapezoidal blade) and *ge* (dagger), as well as some other works of pottery, were placed in the pit. All the objects were found to have suffered different degrees of fire damage. It is apparent that, before they were placed in the pit, they had been burnt and broken along with the animal bones (comprising pig, sheep, goat, cow and oxen bones). Radiocarbon and stratigraphic analysis suggests a date of 13th to 12th centuries BCE (Before the Common Era).

Pit II was also rectangular, with a length of 5.3 metres, a width of 2.3 metres and a depth of 1.68 metres. The collection of objects found here was even richer and included 735 bronzes, 61 gold pieces and 486 jades. In addition, a number of turquoise items, tiger teeth, and cowrie shells were found. The items seem to have been deposited in three layers, rather more systematically than the offerings in Pit I: the bottom layer contained a group of objects of bronze, jade, gold and stone, all small in scale. The bronzes of this layer included animal-face masks (cat. nos 17–19), diamond-shaped fittings (cat. no. 29), small trees (see p. 90) and finials (cat. nos 24–25). The middle layer consisted of objects of bronze of a comparatively larger size, which included a life-size statue (cat. no. 5), 44 heads of varying size (cat. nos 6–10), bronze masks (cat. nos 12–14), masks with protruding eyes (cat. nos 15, 16), a large bronze tree (fig. 1); and some vessels containing cowrie shells and jades. The top layer contained some sixty-odd charred elephant tusks strewn over the other offerings. Most of the objects had been broken and burnt before they were poured into the pit. However, no animal bones were found in this pit. Like the first pit, the earth fill had been pounded hard. Although some of the finds from this pit were similar to those from Pit I, Pit II was distinguished by its enormous number of impressive bronze items. A stylistic evaluation of the bronze objects, as well as stratigraphic and radiocarbon analysis, supports a slightly later date than that of Pit I, that is, 12th to 11th centuries BCE.[1]

The sheer quantity of artefacts from the two pits is incredible and many are of types never seen before. The gold items such as the outer sheathing of a wooden rod traced with designs of fish, birds and human faces, are unique (fig. 2), as are the jades. The jade objects are of various shapes, known by their later names of *zhang* or trapezoidal blade (cat. nos 33, 34), *ge* or dagger (cat. nos 31, 32), *fu* or axe (cat. no. 36) and *zuo* or chisel (cat. no. 37). There are discs with a flange at the inner perimeter, and ritual jade *cong*. Although jade objects such as *zhang* and *ge* are well known Shang types, some of the examples have unusual design features.

The bronze items consist of vessels, bronze replicas of jade discs, and objects hitherto unknown. What most astonished the archaeologists, however, was the group of a hundred bronze figures, heads and masks with fantastic features, amongst them a life-size statue wearing an elaborate robe and standing on a tall square base (cat. no. 5). The figure has two long uplifted arms, and each of its hands forms a circular grip that gives the impression it originally grasped something. There are dozens of life-size heads with large slanting eyes framed by bold outlines, strongly curled nostrils and tight-lipped mouths (cat. nos 2–4, 6–10). Four of such heads were covered with applied gold leaf (cat. no. 7). Some of the same facial features occur on even more extraordinary finds: several large zoomorphic-human masks with enormous ears and long pupils projecting from their eyes (cat. nos 15, 16). There are some equally intriguing animal-face masks (cat. nos 17–19). To this fantastic array of images can be added the fragments of

Figure 1. Bronze tree, late Shang (c. 1200–1100 BCE); height 396 cm; excavated from Sanxingdui Pit II (K2-2: 94).

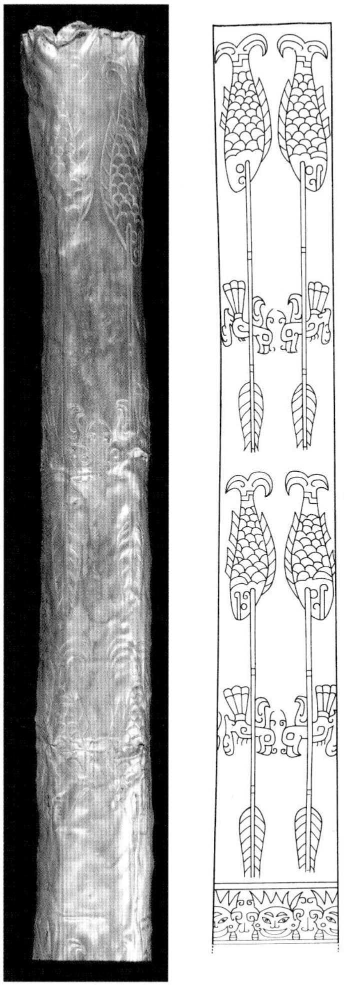

Figure 2. Gold sheathing of a staff, middle Shang (c. 1300–1200 BCE); length 143 cm; excavated from Sanxingdui Pit I (K1: 1).

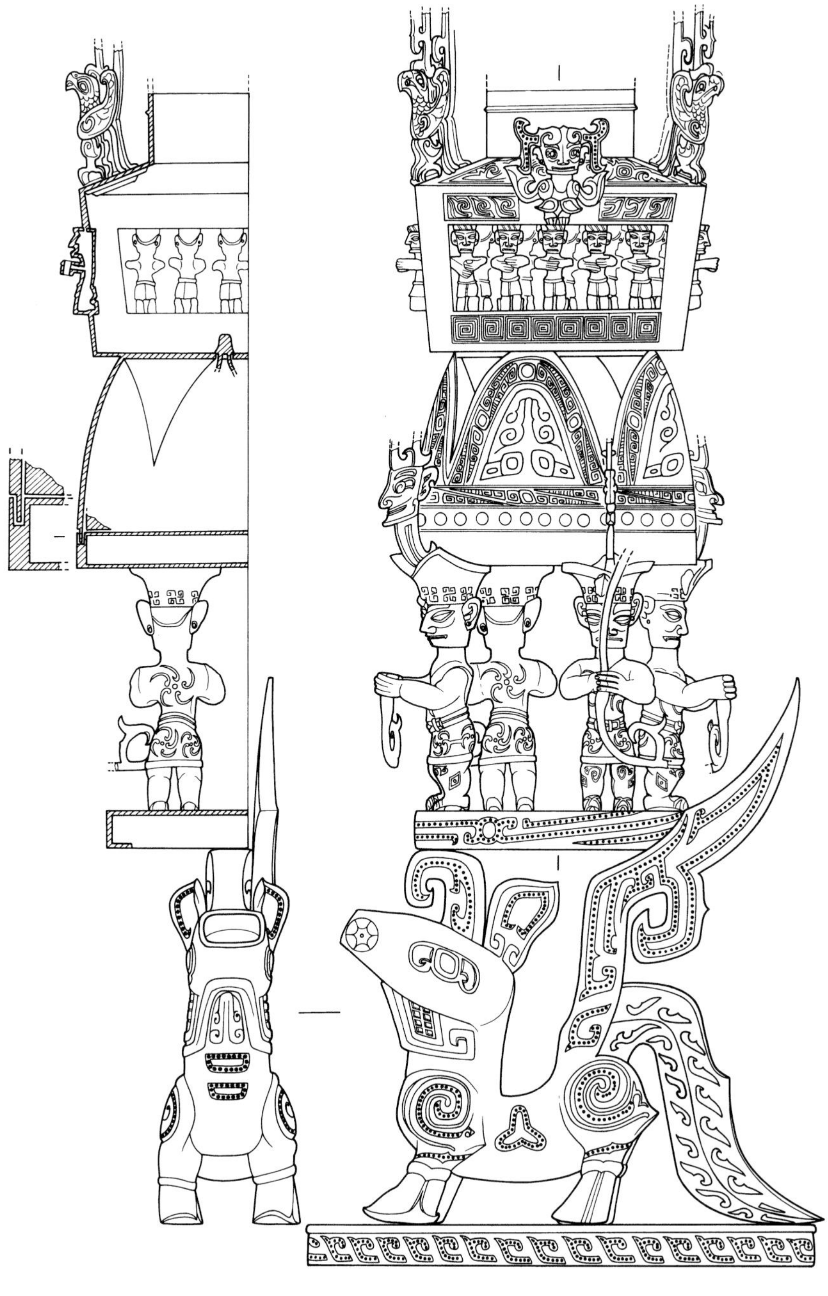

Figure 3. Drawing of the fragment of a large bronze altar, late Shang (c. 1200–1100 BCE); height 53.3 cm; excavated from Sanxingdui Pit II (K2-3: 296).

a large 'altar' with numerous small figures in various postures (fig. 3); also, bronze trees, the largest of which is 396 centimetres high: its curving branches carry leaves, flower buds and small birds (see fig. 1).

The site immediately drew international attention, and the unprecedented forms and scale of the strange images unearthed from the two pits since then have made Sanxingdui world famous.

2. The history of the ancient Shu Kingdom

Contemporaneous with the period when these remarkable objects were buried in the Sanxingdui pits, China was in the late period of the Shang (c. 1600–1100 BCE), the dates of the second dynasty verified by both the rich archaeological finds and the surviving documents written on oracle bones. After several generations of rule and changes of the capital site, King Pangeng (c. 1400 BCE) moved to a new seat of government, a city called Yin in present-day Anyang, Henan province, in northern China. The spectacular cultural relics unearthed at Sanxingdui, a location a thousand kilometres from Anyang, is indeed a startling discovery. It proves that Sanxingdui must have been the centre of an independent local culture, and that the hitherto little known ancient Shu kingdom had probably established its metropolis there.

While the group of unique objects excavated in the two pits indicates that this was a culture civilised enough to rival that which developed in the metropolitan Shang area, the early history of this ancient Shu kingdom for the most part remains a mystery. Unfortunately, there are no contemporary texts or inscriptions documenting or elaborating on the society they came from. Although China's early history began to be well recorded with the emergence of the Shang dynasty, Shu was an area that had not drawn much attention from the Shang kings and the chroniclers of the succeeding Western Zhou dynasty (c. 1100–771 BCE). Texts incised on oracle bones (oracle texts) of the late Shang that provide a view of the world seen exclusively through the eyes of the kings, carry the character 'Shu' several times, but this character has been mainly interpreted as the shadowy title of hostile barbarians, or sometimes as a place attacked by the troops of King Wuding (c. 13th century BCE). Our understanding and reconstruction of the ancient Shu kingdom mainly depends on later literature.

The early history of Shu as described in texts of the Eastern Zhou (771–221 BCE) down to the fourth century CE (Common Era) is rather fragmentary and mixed with legend. *Shibeng* (The pedigree), a text of the Warring Sates period (475–221 BCE) maintains that the history of the Shu can be traced back to Huangdi, and the rulers of Shu were the descendants of this legendary sovereign of ancient China.[2] According to other texts, Huangdi married his son Changyi to a woman from Shu, and their son ascended the throne as the ruler Zhuanxu. In his reign, Zhuanxu appointed one of his descendants to rule the area Shu, thus beginning the period of its history as a kingdom.[3] Such an assertion must have already been a widely accepted view during the Han dynasty (206 BCE – 220 CE). In his memorial to the emperor, the erudite courtier (*boshi*) Chu Shaosun stated that, 'The kings of Shu were the descendants of Huangdi. Nowadays, their descendants still live in the southwest area, five thousand *li* or miles away from the Han [metropolitan area]. They often visit and pay tributes to the court.'[4] Some modern Chinese historians believe that the early history of the Shu as described above, particularly their association with the Huangdi, was probably passed on to the Han historians by the Shu aristocrats while they were visiting the Han capital. It would be difficult to think that such an account of their early history was a forgery, for ancestor worship played an extremely important role in all ancient Chinese societies.[5]

In the literature of the Han and later, accounts of the early history of Shu also mentioned the rulers of the kingdom. Yang Xong (53 BCE – 18 CE) recorded an assertion in *Shuwang bengji* (Biography of the Shu Kings) which listed five names of Shu rulers. They were Cancong, Baiguan, Yufu, Duyu, and Kaiming in succession. Each of the first three dynasties ruled for several hundred years.[6] Modern Chinese historians believe that each dynasty may have had several kings who all shared the same name in their own reigns.[7] Accordingly, Cancong had a pair of unusual eyes (*zongmu* 縱目, meaning vertical or protruding eyes) which gave him credibility as king.[8] It was under Yufu's rule that agriculture was developed. When he died, people established shrines in memory of him. Interestingly, both Baiguan and Yufu's names were homophones of bird's names. The first three dynasties were all based at Qushang, which modern scholars have identified as the Sanxingdui area.[9] Historical accounts from the reign of Duyu were embellished with fanciful details. Duyu is said to have descended from 'heaven' which modern scholars assume may in fact refer to mountains. He appointed himself the Shu king, but soon after extended his title to Wangdi (Emperor Wang). He established his capital at Pi (present-day western Chengdu), and changed his name to Pubei, which again suggested a bird.[10] Chang Qu of the fourth century CE recounts that the last dynasty of Shu, Kaiming, lasted for twelve generations until the kingdom was conquered by the later Emperor Shihuangdi of the Qin in around 316–29 BCE.[11]

Early in *Shangshu* ('Mushi' section), a text compiled during the late Shang to Western Zhou period, the author mentioned that when King Wu (r. c. 1049/45–1043 BCE) set out on a punitive expedition fighting the decisive battle against King Zhou, the last ruler of the Shang dynasty, some ethnic groups, including the Shu, participated in the campaign. Inscriptions on two bronze vessels belonging to an aristocratic family of the late Shang, and excavated at Pengxian near Chengdu, supported such an assertion. Archaeologists believe that the bronzes were either the booty or the reward from the Zhou king for participation in the campaign.[12]

Analysis of these accounts points to several important facts which may help us to understand the Sanxingdui culture and should be stressed here. First, the kingdom of Shu must have been very old, probably established between the Xia (c. 2100–1600 BCE) and Shang periods. Secondly, because of blood-ties with the north, the kingdom had not lived in a historical vacuum, isolated from the cultures of the rest of China. Instead, it had contacts with its far-flung neighbours to the north and east. Thirdly, rituals such as ancestral worship may have played an important part in the life of the community. Finally, it seems that the first three dynastic kings came from the same ethnic group, although probably from different tribes or clans. Duyu, however, was an outsider alien to the indigenous inhabitants.

In the past, these accounts of the early history of Shu were considered nothing more than hearsay.[13] Recent archaeological excavations carried out in Sichuan province, particularly in the Sanxingdui area, however, have begun to throw light on the reliability of these accounts, and to elucidate the mystery surrounding this lost culture.

3. The archaeological excavation at the Sanxingdui site

The existence of a unique and mysterious Shu culture began to be suggested in the early 20th century when some unusual bronze weapons of Shu origin were brought to light.[14] In 1929, an accidental find of nearly four hundred ritual jades by a local farmer at Sanxingdui first indicated that this might be an interesting site. An investigation in 1933 conducted by D.C. Graham, Director of the Huaxi University Museum at the time, revealed that the jades were buried in a rectangular pit 2.1 metres long, 0.9 metres wide and 0.9 metres deep.[15] The village Sanxingdui (lit. The Three Star-Mounds) takes its name from three mounds that look like a constellation in the sky. Modern archaeological investigation in this area began in 1980. All the excavation was done with due attention to stratigraphy and ceramic typology. Soon the archaeologists realised that the three mounds were actually the remnants of the inner wall of an ancient city. A series of subsequent excavations revealed a lost city of some 3.5 square kilometres located south of the Yazi River. The city had been surrounded by a large wall, and the length of surviving sections included: on the east 1,100 metres (originally 1,700 metres), 200 metres on the south and 600 metres on the west. It was wider at the bottom (about 40 metres), narrower at the top (about 20 metres), and was estimated to be around four to ten metres high. The wall was built using a technique whereby layers of earth were rammed between wooden forms and finished with unfired bricks laid on top. The Yazi River to the north may have been used as a natural barrier which could act as a wall. A moat 2.8 metres deep outside the southern wall was also revealed. Based on stratigraphic analysis, and on the evidence of potsherds within it, archaeologists believe that the wall must have been constructed during the early Shang period, and abandoned in the early Zhou dynasty. The buildings inside the wall varied in size, ranging from small houses of 10 square metres to huge halls of 100–200 square metres.

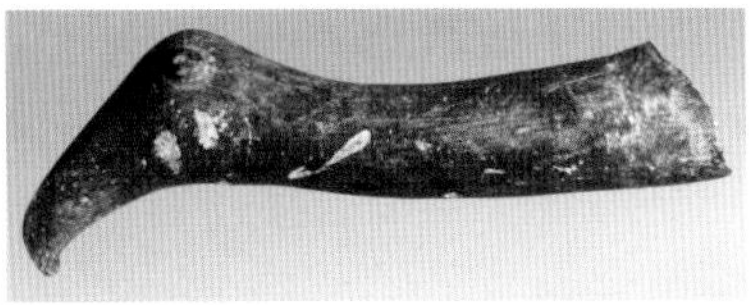

Figure 4. Handle of a pottery dipper resembling a bird's head; Shang (c. 1600–1100 BCE); length 14.09 cm; excavated in 1982 at the Sanxingdui site.

The scale of the city is similar to that of Shangcheng in Henan province, which was one of the largest cities known at the time.

The excavation carried out in this area since 1980 was not only restricted to the city itself, but also extended to a larger area outside. The Sanxingdui site in the broad sense reportedly covered more than 15 square kilometres. Outside the city wall, over 10 groups of sites are scattered nearby, and it is suggested they were satellites of the metropolis. Both tombs and kiln sites were also found. The excavation in this area also revealed a large number of unfinished works in jade and stone, including stocks of raw material, uncut pieces, half-finished items and bits of partially worked materials. This suggests that a major jade industry flourished here. The finds of bronze dross and fragments of baked clay in the Sanxingdui site, which matched the clay core material inside some bronze heads from the two pits, proves all the bronzes were made locally, the foundries located right in the Sanxingdui site.

While the Sanxingdui site was gradually revealing proof of its early occupation, archaeologists were also working on other sites in a broad area around Chengdu which were contemporary with the late Sanxingdui occupation, but reached their height slightly later, during the early Western Zhou period. Interestingly, the ceramic typology suggests that Sanxingdui and Chengdu may represent two distinguishable sub-cultural patterns: while the most representative pottery of the former was a kind of dipper with long handle resembling a bird's head (fig. 4), this was not the case in the latter (instead, here a pottery type with pointed feet was the most typical). On the basis of these excavations, archaeologists suggested that Sanxingdui and Chengdu may have been in succession the centre of the Shu kingdom.[16]

These productive finds also allowed archaeologists to construct a careful and persuasive outline of early Sanxingdui history. The archaeologists have created a four-part periodization for the early occupation of the site, from Neolithic to early Western Zhou. This periodization is derived primarily from the typological examination of ceramic artefacts found within dwelling site strata, supported by stratigraphic analysis and radiocarbon dating. Period 1 is described as late Neolithic, equivalent to the Longshan culture in central China; radiocarbon dates place it as c. 4740–4070 years old. Period 2 is equivalent to the Xia and early Shang dynasties, corresponding in metropolitan China to the occupation of the Erlitou and Zhengzhou sites; radiocarbon dates place it as around 4070–3600 years old. Period 3, to which the Pit I is assigned, is equated with middle Shang or the first half of the Anyang period. The radiocarbon dates place it as 3600–3200 years old. Period 4 is contemporary with the period of the late Shang and the beginning of the Western Zhou. Radiocarbon dating takes it back 3100–2875 years (plus or minus 80 years). Sanxingdui Pit II is assigned to the early part of this period.[17]

This periodization shows an unbroken continuity throughout the occupation of the site. The phase between periods 2 and 3 was considered the most productive, and was a formative and flourishing period for Sanxingdui culture. The decorative patterns on pottery typical of the time emerged and developed into increasingly richer designs. The materials used proved srongly consistent. These two periods form a sharp contrast with period 4 which witnessed a great change in ceramic types and decorative patterns. The emergence of new cultural elements suggests they were accompanied by radical social changes. A dramatic moment that terminated the Sanxingdui occupation occurred during this period. Sanxingdui culture, which had developed for over a thousand years, suddenly died out, whereas the occupation in Chengdu showed rapid growth and prosperity. It seems that the centre of Shu culture had shifted from Sanxingdui to Chengdu. The excavations carried out at Shi'erqiao, Zhihuijie and other sites in Chengdu, where the archaeological strata date from the period of the Shang to the Eastern Zhou, testify to this transformation.[18]

The establishment of the framework of a continuous archaeological history of the Sanxingdui or Shu culture, stretching from Neolithic times to the Western Zhou dynasty, is significant. We can now refine our understanding of the early history of the Shu kingdom by adding a material dimension: we can reconstruct the sequence of dynasties of the kingdom from its very beginning, in close association with the cultural sequence exposed at the Sanxingdui and Chengdu areas. With the aid of recent archaeological achievements, Chinese archaeologists have roughly correlated the strata, ceramic types and other archaeological materials with the chronology of the Shu kings. They assume that period 2 may be associated with the rulers Cancong and Baiguan, who laid the foundation for the growth and prosperity of Sanxingdui culture. The bronzes excavated from the two pits were contemporary with the period of Yufu when Sanxingdui flourished as a material, cultural and political centre. Period 4 is equivalent to that of the late Yufu and early Duyu. During the periods 2 and 3, a type of pottery dipper (see fig. 4) which had become extremely popular, with a long handle resembling a bird-head, was considered to have taken on totemic significance in the context of ancestor worship, for both Baiguan and Yufu may have taken birds as their clan totem (see a further discussion in section 5 of this essay). No cultural phase at the Sanxingdui site witnessed more significant changes than the late period of Yufu, when the destruction of the Sanxingdui occupation occurred. The sudden interruption of consistent settlement at Sanxingdui and the decline of this culture in the area were perhaps the consequence of a violent revolution that resulted in the triumph of Duyu and the shifting of the ritual and political centre from Sanxingdui to Chengdu.[19]

Indeed, the fruitful excavations carried out at the Sanxingdui site, and the archaeologists' efforts to place the once legendary dynasties in a well-developed stratigraphy, establish a firm archaeological context into which the two pits can be fitted.

4. The Sanxingdui Pits

Ever since they were excavated, the purpose or function of the Sanxingdui pits has been the focus of scholarly arguments. It was speculated that the pits might be satellites of some as yet undiscovered tombs (especially, those of Shu kings), but careful search has not located any trace of a burial in the neighbouring area. Only four small tombs had been excavated at the site before the late 1980s. These tombs showed a simple burial arrangement: no valuables were found within them.[20] Another hypothesis held that the pits were the result of some sort of shamanistic practice – once the sacred objects were considered to have outlived their usefulness, or lost their full power, they would be demolished, burnt and buried. Yet it is difficult to imagine why the burial sites included such a wide variety of objects, and among them, numerous less valuable works in stone. A suggestion that the pits were hoards or storage pits is supported by discoveries of several pits at the Sanxingdui site which contained ritual jades. A large number of jade discs *bi* found in 1929, for instance, were piled one on top of another in three levels, as well as *gui* sceptres, *zhang*, *cong*, and *yuan* rings buried in a rectangular pit 2.1 metres long, 0.9 metres wide and 0.9 metres deep. In 1988, an excavation carried out in the northeast of the Sanxingdui site also yielded forty items of stone, bronze and jade, including twenty jade *bi* discs piled one on top of another, just as they were reported to have been in the 1929 find.[21] Such a suggestion, however, does not account for the deliberate breakage of objects or the burnt animal bones in the Sanxingdui pits.[22]

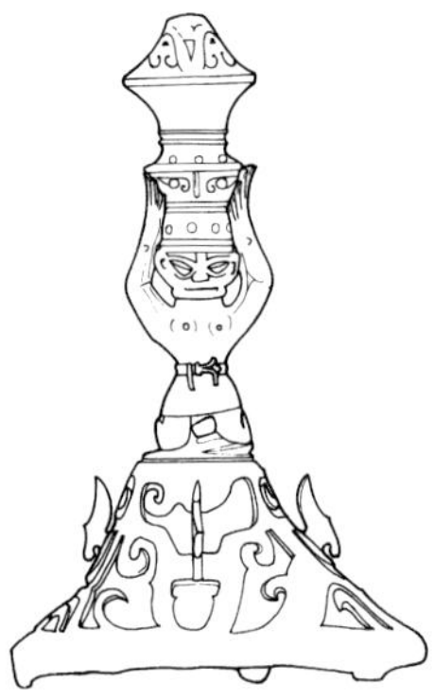

Figure 5. Drawing of a bronze kneeling figure carrying a *zun* vessel on his head; late Shang (c. 1200–1100 BCE); height 15.6 cm; excavated from Sanxingdui Pit II (K2-3: 48).

Figure 6. Bronze kneeling figure with hands holding a trapezoidal blade *zhang*; late Shang (c. 1200–1100 BCE); height 4.7 cm; excavated from Sanxingdui Pit II (K2-3: 325).

Increasingly scholars have come to agree that the Sanxingdui pits were sacrificial pits.[23] The clues to the purpose of these pits are from the contents themselves – the repertoire of types all point to ritual usage, rather than to grave goods or personal ornaments. In addition to the group of bronze figures, heads and masks, the two pits also yielded over four hundred works in bronze, which included vessels, bronze replicas of jade discs, weapons (daggers *ge*) of non-utilitarian function, ornaments and fittings. In addition to the fact that many vessels were found containing cowrie shells and jades, the ritual purpose of these vessels can also be gleaned from a miniature kneeling bronze figure in a posture of dedication who carried a *zun* vessel on his head (fig. 5). Of the more than two hundred and fifty jade and stone works, the most numerous were trapezoidal blades, daggers, chisels and axes or adze, as well as discs, rings, and *cong* ritual jades. None of these objects were made for utilitarian purposes. Clues as to the use of such jades, particularly the blade *zhang*, can be gauged from a tiny bronze figure, and from the engraved scenes on a jade blade *bianzhang*, both from Pit II. The small kneeling figure in bronze holds an object with cleft end upward that is surely meant to be a *zhang* (fig. 6). Engravings on both sides of the *bianzhang* blade show a mountain range and standing or kneeling figures, all crudely arranged (fig. 7). Eight imposing upright *zhang*, among others, stand against a background of mountains. The pictures would seem to represent the scenes of a ritual ceremony. The diversity in types and the abundance in quantity suggest that the objects buried in the two pits reflected the rich repertoire of the cult temples at the state level.

Figure 7. Drawing of a scene on a jade blade *bianzhang*; late Shang (c. 1200–1100 BCE); length 54.2 cm; excavated from Sanxingdui Pit II (K2-3: 201-4).

The use of animal sacrifices also strongly supports the view the pits were used for ritual purposes. Excavations of the pits revealed the burnt offerings of animals, and the burial sites contained some three cubic metres of charred animal bones. A parallel is found elsewhere: many sacrificial pits of the Shang period excavated in northern China showed traces of charred animal bones. Examples have been discovered at eight sites in Henan province, including Sishan, Miaodigou and Erligang.[24]

The way in which the objects were buried also sheds much light on the nature of the Sanxingdui pits. The rectangular pits were carefully and neatly dug. In the case of Pit I, several supplementary channels (80–100 cm wide, 26–34 cm deep) which extended from each side of the pit, according to the archaeologists, may have been imbued with yet unknown significance. It was assumed that the pits were filled at the close of some sort of large-scale sacrificial ceremony on different occasions: animals were killed and burned; the pits were carefully dug; bronzes, jades, elephant tusks, cowrie shells and other valuables were broken and burned, and finally everything was dumped into the pit and buried.

As for the question as to who were the recipients of the sacrificial rites, the scholars have drawn parallels to rituals performed by the Shang court at Anyang, and with rites later defined in the royal ritual texts of the Zhou dynasty. The oracle texts found at Anyang refer frequently to burnt sacrifice and occasionally to the subsequent burial of the sacrificial object. In *Liji* (Record of rites) and *Zhouli* (Rites of the Zhou dynasty) the burnt sacrifices are commonly offered to heaven, the buried offerings to the earth. Some scholars therefore inferred that the Sanxingdui pits might represent sacrifices to nature spirits.[25]

On the other hand, a different opinion holds that the contents of the pit did not reflect carefully prepared offerings, but, instead, deliberate destruction of the highly valuable paraphernalia of the ancestral temples. Such speculation tended to link the sacrificial purpose of the pits to the great disasters of the past that had brought down kings and destroyed the ancestral temples. The deliberate ruin of ritual objects was rather a reflection of the sacrifices made to the owner of those objects by those who took over the kingship.[26]

The suggestion that the pits contained debris buried by the Shang invaders who sacked the city, its palaces and temples is supported by the oracle texts excavated in Anyang which bore the name of Shu as a place attacked by troops of King Wuding. The idea also seems plausible if taking later literature into account, for such destructive behaviour 'to ruin ancestral temples of other states, and to burn and destroy their ritual objects' was a common activity in early Chinese history, and is well documented in pre-Han texts.[27] But the questions are, could Shang troops have ranged as far afield as Sichuan? Why were the two pits of different periods dug at the same location following exactly the same orientations, or why were items buried so neatly, with animal sacrifices, or indeed why would the invaders bury valuable loot at all?

It would therefore appear that the destruction must have been caused by political turmoil or a coup d'etat within the Shu territory. More specifically, the devastation of the temples and the ritual objects was wrought by Duyu, the ruler of the fourth dynasty of Shu, who overthrew the regime of his predecessor Yufu. The sacrificial pits were the symbol of the end of a dynasty, and also a triumphant elegy to the defeated. This hypothesis was based on the close relationship between the archaeological discoveries, the pottery typology, periodization of the early occupation of the site, and the literary accounts of the early history of Shu kingdom, mentioned previously.

Although such speculation does not convincingly answer why there was a gap in time between the two pits – one opinion holds that they should be dated to the same time[28] – it provides at least one comparatively plausible explanation for the mysterious existence of the sacrificial pits at Sangxingdui.

5. The False Face of an Ancient Society

A wide variety of interpretations has been attempted to explain the roles of the Sanxingdui bronzes. Questions have been raised as to whom they represented and what purposes or ritual functions they served. The most puzzling object is the large standing figure, the centrepiece of the whole Sanxingdui find (cat. no. 5). There are no parallels elsewhere, and the figure is the only example of its kind known to exist from that period. On the basis of its enormous scale, exquisite crown and elaborate robe, some scholars conjecture that it may represent the ruler of the kingdom. The crown is especially indicative: figures wearing caps with flared top or with incised paired loop motifs are found on engravings of a gold sheath from Pit I (see fig. 2), and on a bronze head from Pit II (cat. no. 8), yet the crown of the present statue combines the two. The question is, however, if the figure means to represent the image of the ruler, why is he in the posture of someone making offerings? Clues as to the uses of such figures may be gleaned from several other figures discovered in Pit II, which include an incomplete statue with animal headdress (cat. no. 20), a headless figure (fig. 8), and a group of standing figures on an altar fragment (see fig. 3). These figures are of much smaller scale in comparison with the large standing statue, yet they share the same posture, with coiled arms and cupped hands suggesting they were made to hold something. Apparently they were not designed as recipients of ritual offerings, but rather as participants in a ritual drama. The difference between the large figure and the smaller ones is in their costume. However, this may only indicate their position or rank, and not the role they played.

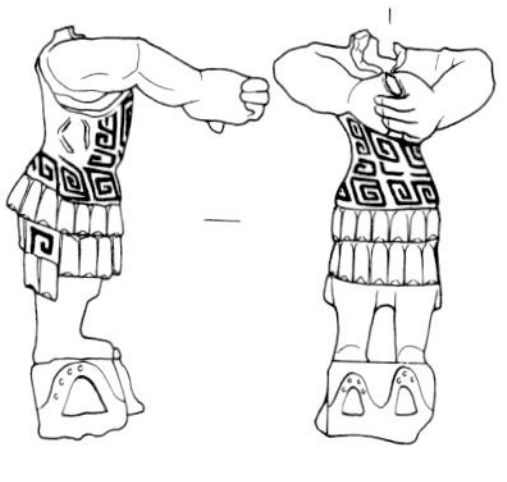

Figure 8. Drawing of a headless bronze figure; late Shang (c. 1200–1100 BCE); height 8.3 cm; excavated from Sanxingdui Pit II (K2-3: 292-2).

In addition to the statue, heads of figures were also found in large numbers. With the exception of one image from Pit I (cat. no. 1), a group of 57 life-size bronze heads from the two pits all show strong, rather schematic human features, including slanting, almond-shaped eyes with the eyeball defined by a horizontal ridge, large brows and the deep sunken grooves below the eyes indicating cheekbones, and a broad, thin-lipped mouth. A sharp right-angled hook behind the ears, extends the jawline and gives a strong impression that the faces are actually covered by masks. This observation is reinforced by the discovery of a group of human masks in Pit II, (cat. nos 12–14) the contour of whose chins is exactly the same.

In accordance with the hypothesis that the large standing figure represented the ruler, it was suggested that the individual heads might in turn represent images of the chiefs of ethnic groups of the Shu kingdom. In keeping with the find that the Sanxingdui site was a metropolitan city surrounded by satellite towns, there also appears to have been a parallel structure of kingship patterns. The different hairstyles of these heads might well be evidence as to their identities.[29] A divergent hypothesis maintains that the heads represented the images of ancestors of different generations to whom sacrifice was being offered.[30] Some scholars speculated that the heads were not the images of deities or the recipients of sacrifice but sacrificial offerings themselves, perhaps even substitutes for decapitated heads. This hypothesis was made on the basis of buried sacrificial offerings uncovered in the Anyang metropolitan area. In 1976 archaeologists excavated at the Anyang royal cemetery 191 sacrificial pits which contained a great number of human victims, mostly beheaded.[31] In addition to human sacrifices, substitutes of figures in stone were also found at Anyang. Therefore there were those who held the opinion that the bronze heads with their necks cut aslant were meant as substitutes for severed heads.[32]

Indeed, the more the mysterious roles of these images were investigated, the more questions were raised. Perhaps a more rewarding line of inquiry is to focus on the central issue of the purpose of the Sanxingdui bronze masks. An examination here of the function of these 'false faces' in the ritual context may bring the ideas behind the bronze images into sharper focus.

On glancing over the Sanxingdui discoveries, one finds that the masks constitute the dominant forms among the bronze human images from the two pits. This impression derives not only from the group of more than thirty masks buried there, but also from the fact that almost all individual heads and free-standing statues were disguised by false faces. Many masks were life-size, but some were only 15 cm high, while others were as high as 66 cm high. The fragments of a damaged mask found in Pit II suggest that the biggest mask could have been as large as 120 cm wide and 80 cm high. Twenty masks from Pit II were characterised by a U-shaped structure when viewed from above (cat. nos 12–14). Judging from the masked heads, the helmet mask, which completely enveloped the head, was also a type used in Sanxingdui (cat. no. 9). Masks found in Sanxingdui pits do not have perforated eye slits, yet small holes were found elsewhere on the sides. All the masks were decorated with pigments, and the remains of black colouring is still visible on areas of the eyes, eyeballs, brows, as well as traces of vermilion on the mouths. Remnants of charred bronze on the earring holes suggest that these masks may have been ornamented with bronze earrings originally.

The masks from Sanxingdui pits range from a schematic representation of human features, to a strange, sometimes gruesome depiction of animal or combined animal and human forms. Whereas the first has a certain degree of realism about it, the latter are stylised to an almost grotesque degree of fantasy.

Masks with human features are seen in a group of 20 masks from Pit II (cat. nos 12–14), as well as in some 57 life-size bronze heads and several figures in standing or kneeling postures that were disguised by a false face (cat. nos 2–10, 20, 21). All these masks show strong, rather schematic human features. The large slanting eyes framed by bold outlines, the deep sunken grooves below the eyes, and the very broad tight-lipped mouth create a surreal quality. Animalistic facial features occur on a group of nine bronze masks discovered at Pit II (cat. nos 17–19). Although they vary in detail, the great round and slightly bulging eyes, geometric headdress, and wide mouth exposing the teeth are particularly prominent features.

A fantastic depiction of combined animal and human forms is represented by three grotesque masks excavated from Pit II (cat. nos 15, 16). These masks share an exceptionally broad and sweeping mouth with the tongue showing in between tightly pursed lips; a sharply protruding chin and emphatic curls defining the nostrils. Even more striking are the enormous projecting ears drawn to sharp tips and the long, slanting eyes from which protrude cylinder-shaped pupils. With its ears, nose, and mouth, it conjures up some strange beast.

Masks in ancient Sanxingdui culture without doubt were primarily associated with ceremonies that had religious significance. The excellent preservation of various characteristics of the masks over long periods of time testifies to their ritual association; according to archaeologists, Pit II is a generation or so later than Pit I, yet the iconic forms of the masks show little change. As consecrated objects imbued with spiritual power, the forms and uses of masks invariably were prescribed by tradition, so it is understandable that stylistic and iconographic innovations in the imagery of masks would be accepted slowly and with reservation. For the mask maker the practice of his art was inconceivable without the existence of the stereotype; he worked chiefly by copying from a previous work, the permissible range of variation from his model limited by the requirements of his cult.

The ritual origin of masks is an almost world wide phenomenon with varied ritual practices in different cultures and societies. In general, two important classes of masks may be distinguished: those worn by the living and masks of the dead.[33] Although we have no evidence that Sanxingdui masks were made for the deceased, there is little doubt that masks were worn in ritual ceremonies. The dozens of individual heads and several figures in various postures from the two pits provide vivid examples of how the masks worked. Undoubtedly, masked ritual played a vital role in community life of the ancient Sanxingdui inhabitants.[34]

The use of a mask was intended to identify the wearer with the figure he represented. Early Western Zhou ritual texts such as *Liji* recorded an old tradition of using the representative of the deceased (called *shi* 尸, corpse) in a ceremony dedicated to ancestors. The *shi* was generally a close, young relative who wore a costume (possibly including a mask) reproducing the features of the dead person. The *shi* was an impersonator, that is, a person serving as a reminder of the ancestor to whom sacrifice was being offered. During such a ceremony, the impersonator was much more than an actor in a drama. Although the exact meaning may have been different, the group of Sanxingdui masked figures in bronze all have the character of an impersonator. It is likely the masks were used to impersonate and identify with certain supernatural beings in order to effect some communal good. Their identity as the participants or impersonators in a sort of grandiose ritual ceremony is further supported by their varying forms and postures: amongst the discoveries there are standing figures with lifted arms and hands cupped in front to hold an offering (cat. no. 5, 20; fig. 8); there are kneeling figures in a reverent attitude with hands resting on their thighs or carrying a ritual vessel on the head (cat. no. 21; fig. 5). The role of these figures in bronze seems twofold: while they are the recurrent images of a cult that involved a masked ceremony, they also served in a fetish role. In a ritual ceremony, to put on a mask representing a mythological figure or spiritual force is to become that figure or force. A magico-religious transformation is brought about by wearing a mask.

This fetish character is certainly the case with the giant bronze masks (cat. nos 12, 15, 16). To perform a ritual dance while carrying one of such huge masks was not simply the matter of an athletic feat, but the expression of the imagination. It is also interesting to note that, almost all the masks have a pair of square holes at the sides. The purpose of these holes was perhaps to attach the masks to part of a building or a support structure in some other material. In some cases, a square hole on the forehead was chiselled out (cat. nos 13, 15). If the hole was not meant to secure an attachment, it must have been used to insert ornamental fittings as seen on a mask with ornamented forehead and protruding pupils (cat. no. 16).

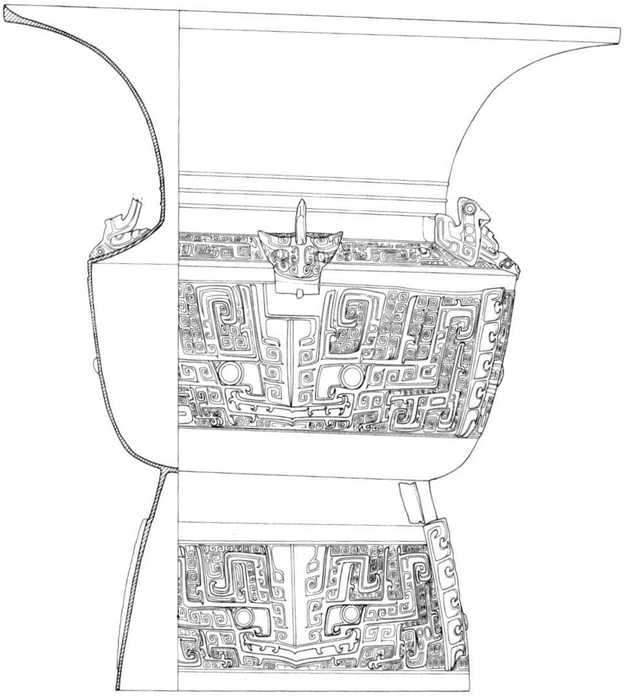

Figure 9. Drawing of a bronze vessel *zun*; late Shang (c. 1200–1100 BCE); height 44.2 cm; excavated from Sanxingdui Pit II (K2-2: 79).

Religions, in the form of ancestor-worship, may have been one of the main principles behind mask making among the people of Sanxingdui; and some masks were probably designed to represent ancestors. As is common to all ancient agricultural societies, the symbolism of the plant and seed, representing regrowth, determined their conception of the world, and their art stemmed from this world view.[35] In ancient Chinese art, statues portray ancestors, masks represent the spirits of dead forbears, and paintings and decorative arts employ the same motifs over and over again. All representations of ancestors are the media through which the forbears speak to the present generation.

Attempts have been made to connect the large masks with protruding eyes (cat. nos 15, 16) with Cancong, the first ruler of the Shu kingdom. As mentioned earlier, Cancong was known in later literature for his pair of unique eyes called *zongmu*. The term was usually taken to mean 'vertical eyes' which described a common attribute of deities in Chinese myth and folklore. The cylindrical eyes of the Sanxingdui masks, however, suggest another meaning of the word – 'protruding eyes'. Indeed, if there does exist a link between an ancestor, the bronze image, and the veneration for eyes, *zongmu* may actually refer to the protruding eyes which constitutes this association. Support for such speculation comes also from the epigraphic form of the word 'Shu', used by the Shang to indicate the kingdom and the people who lived in the modern Sichuan area. In oracle texts Shu is written as [glyph], which shows an enormous eye with a serpentine body. Besides, the character 'Qu' 瞿 which was used to name the capital city Cancong, Baiguan and Yufu and was identified as Sanxingdui by scholars, is written in the form of a big bird topped by a pair of tremendous eyes. The Han dynasty *Shuwen* dictionary defines the character as the 'gaze of an eagle or a falcon-like bird'. Again, epigraphy appears to build up a possible link between the art forms (birds, protruding eyes) and their iconography (ancestral worship).

Whether or not the masks with protruding eyes depicted Cancong is still open to question. However, there is strong evidence to suggest that ancestor worship was a very important motivation behind the Sanxingdui art. This can be gleaned from a specific motif, the bird, which has been one of the most popular animal subjects in Sanxingdui art.

Many important ritual objects in both bronze and jade excavated from the two pits bear the bird motif. It is seen, for instance, on the large altar fragment (see fig. 3). Most of the ritual vessels of the *zun* and *lei* type have small, flat birds on their shoulders (fig. 9). A bird is contained within the open work on the tip of a ceremonial trapezoidal blade *zhang* (fig. 10). The bird motif was cast in large sculptures as exemplified by a magnificent bird's head (cat. no. 23) and designed as small bell finials (fig. 11). Among the most meaningful works with the bird motif are several bronze trees, or 'spirit-trees' as archaeologists have termed them, the largest of which is nearly four metres tall (see fig. 1). It has nine gracefully curving branches emerging from the trunk at different levels, supporting leaves and flower buds. Seated on nine of these buds are nine birds with hooked beaks – the feature gives one an impression that it might better be called a 'bird tree'. A schematic dragon, originally reaching to the top of the tree from the base, is now only preserved in part at the lower half. The enormous scale and elaborate construction of such bronze trees – some fruit finials were even covered with gold leaf on their fruiting branches[36] – indicate that they must have played an important role in the ritual life of Sanxingdui inhabitants.

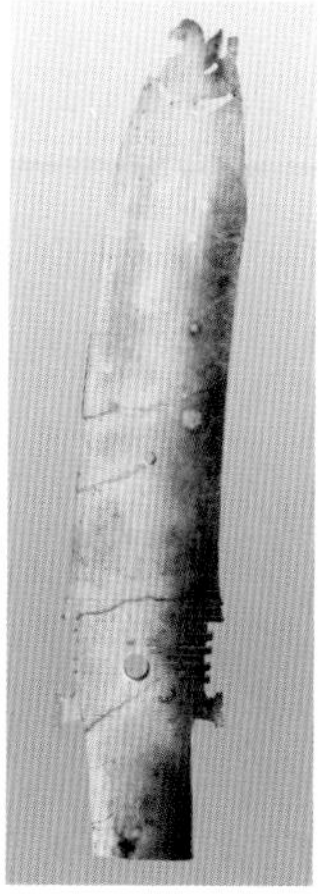

Figure 10. Jade ceremonial trapezoidal blade *zhang*; middle Shang (c. 1300–1200 BCE); length 38.2 cm; excavated from Sanxingdui Pit I (K1: 235-5).

Figure 11. Bronze bell finial; late Shang (c. 1200–1100 BCE); height 14 cm; excavated from Sanxingdui Pit II (K2-2: 103-8).

The examples given above establish that the people of Sanxingdui were favourably inclined towards a particular animal – the bird. The prevalence of the motif may further indicate that the bird was of near totemic importance in Sanxingdui art, and its significance for the welfare of the society stemmed from its role in the veneration of the ancestors.

With the belief that everything in nature possessed a spirit, men in antiquity legitimised their own authority by identifying with a specific non-human spirit. They would adopt a creature in nature, trace their ancestry back to the chosen object, then select the animal as the emblem of themselves and their clan. This is totemic practice, one which consolidates family pride and distinguishes social lines.[37] Totemism was widespread in ancient Chinese society. In Chinese myths, animals often play roles as the progenitors of whole groups of people. It is the belief of some historians that nine out of ten of the ancient sages in Chinese legends were versions of animal deities; others think that many mythological and legendary heroes were in reality chiefs of ethnic and social groups which claimed animals as their totemic ancestors.[38] Such totemism may have also formed a significant part in the religious life of the ancient Sanxingdui people, and is reinforced by the rich archaeological finds in the area and supported by the literary accounts.

Anthropologists have differentiated between group (social or collective) and individual totemism and claimed that the former is the most widely disseminated form. The general characteristics include essentially the following: the mystical association of animal and plant species to the groups; the names of groups that can be based either directly or indirectly on the totem; the hereditary transmission of the totems; and the totemistic emblems, symbols, and taboo formulas which are common to the entire group. Archaeological finds in Sanxingdui and the literary records related to the early history of the Shu accord surprisingly with this definition.[39]

As previously mentioned, both the names of Baiguan and Yufu, rulers of the second and third dynasties of the Shu kingdom, are homophones of bird names. 'Yufu' is identified with the cormorant or other predatory aquatic bird. Probably in an effort to secure spiritual sanction for the mandate of his new dynasty, Duyu, the successor to Yufu, changed his name to Pubei which was also the name of a species of bird.[40] He was very successful in doing so; even today, Duyu's name is closely associated with a species of bird, the *dujuan* or cuckoo. Chinese believe that the bird represents his noble spirit, and the bird's sad voice speaks of the sorrows of parting. During period 2, and particularly period 3 of the early Sanxingdui occupation which has by association been connected with Baiguan and Yufu's reigns, a type of pottery dipper with a long handle resembling a bird's head became extremely popular (see fig. 4). Pottery pieces of this type were seldom found elsewhere in Sichuan and died out completely after the decline of the Sanxingdui occupation in the early Western Zhou. The interesting finds have led archaeologists to believe that there must have been some mystical, reverential, and genealogical relationship of the Sanxingdui inhabitants with this motif.[41] It is possible that the bird has served as the emblem or symbol of a kinship group in Sanxingdui, and the reason for the popularity of such pottery was the close and vital relationship between the 'totem' and the clan. Although no accounts of its origin are available, it appears that the totem had a connection with the primitive economic structure of the ethnic group who resided in the area. According to historians, even during Yufu's time (i.e., roughly period 3 of the Sanxingdui occupation), the Chengdu plain for the most part was still marshland.[42] Fishing was probably an important source of livelihood for the community and the bird, a cormorant or other predatory aquatic bird, would be viewed as a helper or a companion. Birds were gradually deified and became a relative, a protector, and a progenitor or a totem of the people of Shu.

It is worth noting that many of the birds in Sanxingdui art were designed to have the features of a cormorant or other predatory aquatic bird, with a hooklike beak and accompanied fish motifs. Pit I yielded a group of ceremonial trapezoidal blade *zhang* with a notched tip that turns the blade into a gaping fish (fig. 12). An object full of significance is a tube of sheet gold discovered in Pit I (see fig. 2). Judging from the remains of carbonised wood inside, the staff had probably formed the outer sheathing of a wooden rod. The upper third of its length is engraved with two human heads wearing crowns, and two groups each composed of a pair of birds and two fish with feathered arrows lodged in their heads. The birds show cormorant-like features with hooklike beaks. The engraving seems to depict a hunting or fishing scene featuring a display of arrows and predatory aquatic birds, and a rod or staff of kingship, which would indicate a very precious object with prestige value. The images depicted on it are therefore imbued with important messages. One can not help but link the scene with Yufu, the third ruler of the Shu kingdom.

The bird motif occurs on other significant finds: a bronze human figure with bird's feet (cat. no. 22), and several bronze birds with human faces (cat. no. 24). Preserved only in fragment, the former consists of two parts: a human body with bird's feet on the top and two birds below. The exquisite decoration on the figure's skirt indicate its prestigious identity. The tiny birds with human faces or masks which were used as finials of a bronze tree were crowned. The same human-headed bird appeared on a large altar fragment in bronze which has been recognised by archaeologists as the centre piece of an assumed cult temple in Sanxingdui (see fig. 3). Presenting a solemn frontal pose, it stood at the centre of the fragmentary remains, symmetrically flanked by a pair of birds. Below, arranged in rows on different levels, stood human figures in a reverent pose with uplifted arms and hands coiled in front as if to grasp something. The importance of the human-headed bird is evident from its location and its central and symmetrical arrangement.

Figure 12. Jade ceremonial trapezoidal blade *zhang*; middle Shang (c. 1300–1200 BCE), length 42.5 cm, excavated from Sanxingdui Pit I (K1:06)

Obviously, a bird of totemic significance featured heavily in the religion and magical practices of the ancient Shu culture. The sense of a close bond between man and these creatures led to an anthropomorphising of the birds. The birds were not only considered as living beings but were humanised to such an extent that the distinction between man and bird became virtually lost. They may have acted as intermediaries to help people communicate with the spirit realm.

The function of the Sanxingdui masks was probably multiple. In addition to fulfilling a fetish role, the false faces could possibly represent demonic spirits, with apotropaic value. Such an impression is aroused by the group of animal masks (cat. nos 17–19). Aggressive supernatural spirits of an almost demonic nature are represented on these masks. They remind us of the *taotie* animal face – the most popular motif on ritual objects of Bronze Age China that was also employed as decoration on bronze vessels in Sanxingdui (see fig. 9). As to the *taotie*, many interpretations have been offered,[43] but one early tradition referred to it as the image of a harmful spirit.[44] The depiction of these demons on ritual vessels allowed people to familiarise themselves with their appearance, to forewarn them should they encounter these spirits abroad. The theory behind this belief was that a danger confronted through a visual image gave protection against it. To some extent, the idea behind the *taotie* motif as interpreted by the author of *Zuozhuan*, relates to a kind of mask ceremony called *nuo* 儺 which is primarily concerned with exorcism. In such a ceremony, masks of grotesque appearance were used to drive away pestilences and harmful spirits. Some masks with hideous features in

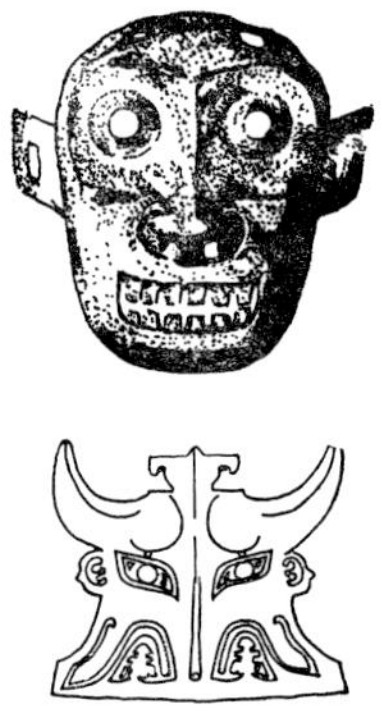

Figure 13. Drawings of bronze masks; Shang dynasty; human mask height 16.5 cm, width 17.7 cm; animal mask height 16–18 cm, width 18–19 cm; excavated in Chenggu, Shaanxi province.

Figure 14. Drawing of miniature replica of the mask; height 7.8 cm, width 6 cm; Shang dynasty; excavated in Laoniupo, Shaanxi province.

Figure 15. Drawing of a seated figure in stone with a large animal head or mask; late Shang or early Zhou period; height 9 cm, width 13.5 cm; excavated in Luanping, Hebei province.

fact represented evil forces that can be neutralised or exorcised by dance-ceremonies and performances of rites. The *nuo* ceremony was well documented in Western Zhou ritual texts such as *Liji*, and its origin can be traced back to Shang times as proved by pictorial writings in oracle text relating to masks found at Anyang. One of such character is [illegible], which Chinese scholars have interpreted as the pictorial form of an exorcist driving away the harmful spirits from home.[45] The exorcist may have to wear a mask called *qi* 魌, written in oracle text as [illegible]. The character vividly resembles a man with a mask that has perforated eye slits. Another character *gui* [illegible], denoting spirits or demons, also takes the form of a man disguised by a mask. The pictorial form suggests that the harmful spirit to be exorcised may have also been represented by a hideous mask. This character illustrates how man's identity can be changed, or a magico-religious transformation could be brought about by wearing a mask. Interestingly, the Shang ritual activity involved in the use of masks as described in oracle texts and later literature is borne out by archaeological discovery. From 1955 to 1976, fifty-nine life-sized masks from the Shang dynasty were excavated in Chenggu, Shaanxi province, a neighbouring district of the ancient Shu territory where the influence of both Shu and Shang cultures is equally strong.[46] Those masks ranged from hideous representations of human faces to grotesque animal forms (fig. 13). Miniature replicas of masks with similar features were also discovered in Shang tombs at Laoniupo in Shaanxi province (fig. 14).[47] Two other sculptures of the late Shang or early Zhou period, a seated figure in stone with a large animal head that has been assumed to be a mask, excavated in Luanping, Hebei province (fig. 15),[48] and a small bronze human head under a *taotie* like animal mask, formerly in the Avery Brundage collection (fig. 16),[49] provide tangible evidence for the cult under discussion.

There is no actual proof that the art of the mask in Shu developed out of the metropolitan Shang culture which flourished in northern China. However, the people of Shu did not live in a historical vacuum, isolated from the cultures of the rest of China. The metropolitan Anyang influences were absorbed and adapted to a very great extent as mentioned earlier. During the Han dynasty, the *nuo* ceremony was reported as still popular in the Sichuan area. A type of pottery masked figure excavated from the Eastern Han (25–220 CE) tombs, showing grotesque or hideous facial features, was identified as Fangxiang, a famous exorcist recorded in early Western Zhou dynasty ritual texts.[50]

Whatever these zoomorphic masks represent, however, it is certain that the people of Sanxingdui used animal disguises as a means to raise the mask-wearer to a supernatural state. The idea is clearly seen in a figure wearing a mask with an animal headdress (cat. no. 20). The grotesque, or even gruesome features of the masks signify a general function of masks common to all cultures: they were used to evoke certain reactions in the beholder, such as awe of the deified figure it represented or fear of harmful spirits. As the appearance of an unusual form at a ritual ceremony would have attracted attention and highlighted the meaning implied in the ritual activities, the Sanxingdui bronze figures were designed to greatly emphasise the power of eyes. They signify a particular notion of the eye as a physical entity, transformed by art into an alien form to inspire awe.[51]

Figure 16. A small bronze human head under a *taotie* like animal mask; late Shang or early Western Zhou period; formerly in the Avery Brundage collection.

It is possible that masks created by the people of Sanxingdui and the religious aspects associated with them embraced the whole community life and fulfilled a multitude of functions. What is discussed here are just a few of the possibilities. Although the research on the Sanxingdui site will occupy archaeologists and historians for years to come, the find of a civilised early Bronze Age in Sichuan is remarkably important, not only for the gap it fills in our knowledge of the early history of the Shu kingdom, but also for the expansion of our definition of the 'Shang civilisation'.

Notes

1. For the excavation of Sanxingdui pits, see Sichuan Provincial Administration for Cultural Relics, et al. 10 (1987), 5 (1989); Bagley (1988, 1990); Institute of Archaeology of Sichuan Province (1999).
2. Cited in Sima Zhen's (Tang) annotation of *Shiji* (Records of the historian) by Sima Qian (145–86 BCE), *juan* 13. For the date of *Shibeng*, see Li Xueqing (1997), p. 206. Huangdi is one of the *wudi* or Five Sovereigns in earliest Chinese history. The time of *wudi*, according to some Chinese scholars, is equivalent to the late Yangshao culture (c. 4800–3000 BCE) and into the period of the Longshan culture (c. 2500–2000 BCE).
3. *Puji* (Record of the Pedigree), cited in Zhang Shoujie's annotation of *Shiji*, *ibid*. This assertion was also recorded in some pre-Han texts, such as *Dadai liji*, a chapter of 'Dixi (The pedigree of the sovereigns)', and *Shanhaijing* (Classic of the Mountains and Seas), *juan 18*, 'Haineijing', etc.
4. *Shiji*, *ibid*.
5. Meng Wentong (1981), pp. 36–38; Li Xueqing (1997), pp. 204–223.
6. The text survives in Yan Kejun et al., ed. *Quan shanggu sandai Qin Han Sanguo Liuchao wen* (A Complete Edition of Literature from Antiquity, from the Qin, Han, Three Kingdoms and Six Dynasties), completed in 1836, Beijing: Zhonghua Press, 1987, reprint. While some scholars doubt its Han date, others put it even earlier. See Meng Wentong (1981).
7. Li Xueqing (1997), p. 207.
8. This assertion was recorded in Chang Qu (4th century CE), *Huayang guozhi* (Records of the Huayang Kingdom) [annotated by Ren Naiping, Shaihai: Guji Press, 1987], a chapter entitled *Shuji* (Records of Shu).
9. See Xu Chaolong, in Li Shaoming et al. ed. (1993), pp. 275–284.
10. See Yang Xiong's *Shuwang bengji*, and Chang Qu's *Huayang guozhi*.
11. Chang Qu, *ibid*.
12. Xu Zhongsu, 'Sichuan pengxian mengyangzhen chutu de yindqai er zhi' (Two Bronze Vessel *zhi* of the Shang Dynasty Excavated at Mengyang, Pengxian County in Sichuan), *Wenwu*, 6 (1962), pp. 15–18.
13. The renowned historian Gu Jiegang was the most representative, see his article: ' Gudai Bashu yu zhongyuan de guanxi shuo jiqi pipan' (A Critical Reappraisal of the Relationship of Ancient Ba-Shu and Central China), *Zhongguo wenhua yanjiu huikan* (Journal of the Chinese Cultural Studies), vol. 1, September, 1941.
14. Wei Juxian, 'Bashu wenhua' (The Culture of Ba and Shu), *Shuowen Monthly*, vol. 3, no. 4, 1942.
15. D.C. Graham (1936).
16. Song Zhimin (1989); Luo Kaiyu (1989), and Zhao Dianzeng (1992).
17. Sichuan Provincial Administration for Cultral Relics, et al. (1987); Bagley (1988), pp. 83–4; Chen Xiandan

(1989); Zhao Dianzeng (1992), pp. 3–12; Chen De'an, et al. (1998), pp. 3–4.
18. See Sichuan Provincial Administration for Cultural Relics, et al., 12 (1987), and The Museum of Sichuan University (1987).
19. For a detailed discussion, see Xu Chaolong (1992, 1993); Hu Changyu and Cai Ge (1992); Zhao Dianzeng (1992).
20. See Sichuan Provincial Administration for Cultural Relics, et al., 2 (1987).
21. Zhao Dianzeng, in J. Rawson (1996), p. 235.
22. For discussions on the two pits, see Lin Xiang (1987); Chen Xiandan (1989); Sun Hua (1993).
23. See Institute of Archaeology of Sichuan Province (1999), 438–448.
24. See Bu Gong, 'Cishan jisikeng yizhi ji xiangguan mengt' (A Sacrificial Pit at Cishan and Related Questions), *Wenwu*, 11 (1987), pp. 43–47.
25. See Qu Xiaoqiang et al. (1993), pp. 229–239.
26. See Xu Chaolong (1992, 1993); Institute of Archaeology of Sichuan Province (1999).
27. Such destructive behaviour is well documented in many pre-Han classics such as *Guoyu* (in *Zhouyu* section), *Mengzi* (*zhang* 11), *Mozi* (*juan* 3), and *Lushi Chunqiu*.
28. Hu Changyu and Cai Ge (1992).
29. Qu Xiaoqiang (1993), pp. 94–100.
30. Institute of Archaeology of Sichuan Province (1999): 443.
31. See Anyang Excavation Team, 'Anyang Yinxu nuli jisikeng de fajue' (The Excavation of the Slave Sacrificial Pits at the Yin Site in Anyang), *Kaogu*, 1 (1977), pp. 20–36.
32. Sichuan Provincial Administration for Cultural Relics, et al., 10 (1987); Li Shaoming, et al. (1993), pp. 107–108.
33. For studies on ritual masks, see J. Gregor, *Masks of the World*, London, 1936; Oto Bihalji-Merin, *Masks of the World*, London: Thames & Hudson, 1971; Andreas Lommel (1972); Henry Pernet, *Ritual Masks: Deceptions and Revelations*, trans., by Laura Grillo, Columbia: University of South Carolina Press, 1990.
34. Childs-Johnson discussed the Shamanistic character of these masks, see her article, 2 (1989): 65–68.
35. See Andreas Lommel, *ibid.*, p. 9.
36. Institute of Archaeology of Sichuan Province (1999), p. 227.
37. For studies of Totemism, see Claude Lévi-Strauss (1964), and J. G. Frazer, *Totemica: A Supplement to Totemism and Exogamy*, London, 1937.
38. A summary of this view is found in K.C. Chang, *Early Chinese Civilisation*, Cambridge, Mass: Harvard University Press, 1976, p. 175.
39. Ralph Piddington offers a short but sufficient characterisation of totemic phenomena. See *An introduction to social anthropology*, Edinburgh: Oliver and Boyd, 1950, vol. 1, pp. 200–206.
40. Xu Chaolong (1993), p. 280.
41. Hu Changyu and Cai Ge (1992); Zhao Dianzeng (1992).
42. Ren Naiqiang (1986), p. 69.
43. For recent studies on this subject, see K. C. Chang (1984): 61–80; Robert Bagley (1987): 17–24; Ladislav Kesner (1991): 30–34; Elizabeth Childs-Johnson (1998): 5–172.
44. See the chapter of 'The third year of Duke Xuan' in *Zuozhuan*, a text compiled during the Warring States period (476–221 BCE). The text says that *ding* tripods were cast to bear images and that the purpose of these representations was to enable people to distinguish divine from evil. The motif referred to is most probably the *taotie* mask, since this motif was the most prominent image in the decoration of early bronze vessels. The text may only concern the 'evil' aspect of the *taotie*, since the author explains the main benefit of these images on the tripods was as a forewarning against evil spirits abroad.
45. Yu Xingwu (1983).
46. See Tang Jinyu et al. (1980); Li Boqian (1983); Zhu Peizhang, et al., 'Shaanxi sheng Chenggu, Baoji, Lantian chutu heshouji de qingtongqi' (Bronzes Excavated and Collected from Chenggu, Baoji and Lantian in Shaanxi Province), *Wenwu*, 1 (1966), pp 1–3.
47. Dept of Archaeology, Northwest University, 6 (1988).
48. Zhao Zhihou, 'Hebei Luanping xian Yingfang cun chutu shoumian shiren' (A Stone Figure with Animal Face Discovered at Yingfang Village in Luanping, Hebei Province), *Wenwu*, 2 (1985), p. 93.
49. Bradley Smith & Wan-go Weng, *China: A History in Art*, Gemini Smith Inc. (1979), p. 33.
50. Yu Dezhang, 'Sichuan fangxianyong xiaokao' (A Preliminary Examination of the Han Tomb Figure Fangxiang from Sichuan), *Chengdu wenwu*, 3 (1988), pp. 12–14.
51. For a discussion on the significance of the eyes in Sanxingdui bronzes, see Wu Hong (1997).

藏在假面具後的古蜀文化

1986年7月，在四川成都附近廣元縣一個叫三星堆的地方，當地磚瓦廠工人掘磚土時，意外地挖出了埋在兩個長方形坑中的上千件青銅器，金器，玉器和石器。這個意外發現變成了20世紀中國最重要的考古成果之一。一號坑長4.64米，寬3.48米，深1.64米。在420件發掘品中，有178件青銅器，4件金器，129件玉器，70件石器，39件陶器。此外，坑中還有13根象牙，及3立方米左右的動物骨渣。二號坑長5.30米，寬2.30米，深1.68米，從中共發掘出735件青銅器，61件金器，486件玉器。跟一號坑相比，二號坑不僅藏物豐富，而且掩埋層次更爲清晰：底層主要是玉器與小型青銅器，中層堆放大型青銅器，有立人像，頭像，面具等；上層是60余根象牙。兩個坑中所有的器物在被掩埋之前，都曾被砸爛，焚燒。據測定，一號坑相當於商代中期，約公元前13-12世紀，二號坑相當於商代晚期，在公元前12-11世紀左右。三星堆文物的發掘震驚了世界，也引發了一波探討古蜀文明的熱潮。

關於古蜀歷史，正史記載甚少，安陽出土的商末甲骨文偶有"蜀"字出現，但大多是作爲被商王征伐之地。根據戰國以降史籍中的零星記載，古蜀國歷史可以追溯到黄帝。據説黄帝的一個兒子昌意與蜀女子結婚，他們的兒子高陽成爲帝顓頊，再封其子孫於蜀，從此開始了蜀作爲一個方國的歷史。歷代蜀王有蠶叢，柏灌，魚鳧，杜宇和開明。每個王朝或許歷經數位統治者，但都使用同一個稱號。柏灌和魚鳧的名字都於鳥有關。魚鳧死後，蜀人思之，爲立祠。關於杜宇，古籍記載用神話筆法説他乃從天而降，這彷佛在暗示他是個外來户。而且他即位後馬上就遷了都。

以往，古籍中關於古蜀歷史的敘述，曾被懷疑爲無稽之談。然而，近年來碩果累累的考古發掘，證明古人所記不僅僅是傳説而已。早在20年代初，當一些造型紋飾奇特的青銅兵器在四川出現，人們便開始詢問是否存在著一個獨特的古蜀文化。1929年，當地農民在三星堆意外挖出的四百多件玉器，證明這里是一個有重大考古價值的遺址。從1980年以來考古工作者所進行的一系列發掘，逐漸揭開了一個被歲月湮沒的古城的秘密。這個古城，北面以河流爲障，其余三面圍以高約4-6米，基寬40余米的夯土城牆，城内面積達3.5平方公里，是已知當時最大城市之一。根據地層迭壓關係，考古學家推測城牆始建於商代早期，至西周初期被廢棄。在古城外方圓15平方公里範圍内，還發現密集的居住區，窯址，未完工的玉石料。所有這些都證明三星堆曾經是一個繁榮一時的區域性的政治經濟中心。根據這十多年來科學發掘所獲得的地層關係及碳14測年數據，考古學家將三星堆文化大略上分爲四期。一期相當於新石器時代晚期，距今4740-4070年左右；二期與夏代及商代前期對應，距今4070-3600年左右；三期時代約在商代末期到西周初期，距今3100-2875左右。

三星堆一，二號坑的發現，朝揭開古蜀文明的秘密，又邁進了一大步。然而對這兩個坑的性質，學術界依然沒有定見。有人推測它們是蜀王大墓的一部分，但是周圍並沒有發現任何墓葬的痕跡。一種看法説它們是窖藏，可是卻沒有回答爲何坑中的器物曾被砸爛，焚燒。另一種建議認爲它們是"厭勝"的結果-神像不靈因而被毀壞，丢棄-這種説法忽略了坑中所埋，有許多並不是很貴重的石器。學術界現在傾向於認爲這兩個坑是祭祀坑，因爲坑中所埋，全都不是實用的器皿，也非個人飾物。埋葬時使用動物之類的犧牲，器物投入層次分明，坑兩邊還挖出規整的輔助坑道，所有這些都説明它們跟祭祀有關。

至于祭祀活動爲誰而舉行，學術界也看法不同。一種意見引證周代禮書，認爲焚燒掩埋祭品，所祭對象定是天地之類的自然神祇。持反對意見者認爲，所埋器物其實是國家宗廟的全套像設，由于人禍而遭毀壞埋葬。受祭對象不是别人，而是器物的主人。很有可能三星堆古城的毀滅，是商王大軍屠城的結果，因爲安陽出土的甲骨文多次提及伐蜀之舉。可問題是，入侵者眞能遠及處於西南邊陲的三星堆？爲什麼兩個祭祀坑相隔百年，卻挖在同一方位，且挖得這麼整齊？爲什麼入侵者不帶走珍貴的戰利品？另一種意見因此提出，“外來户”杜宇可能是這場悲劇的導演，三星堆都城的廢棄，宗廟的被毀，是杜宇改朝換代的結果。考古學家發現，三星堆文化第二，三期流行的與柏灌，魚鳧有關的鳥頭柄勺，在商末周初的第四期完全消失。與此同時，蜀文化在成都地區趨向繁榮。當時的情形可能是，杜宇滅魚鳧，毀宗廟，將政治中心遷移到成都地區去了。

三星堆文物中，最醒目的要數面具。這種印象不僅來自那三十余件青銅面具，而且還由于所有青銅頭像和立人像，絶大多數都戴有假面。這些面具大小不一，形式各異。有的長方形，有的包裹整個頭部。其面部表情，從夸張的人面，到半人半獸的形象，乃至純粹的獸面，無不給人儼峻冷漠的印象。有三件人獸面相結合的假面，眼球呈柱狀凸出，令人望而生畏。

毫無疑問，假面具與古代三星堆居民的祭祀活動關係密切。最直接的證明，來自那彷佛是規範化的面容。兩個祭祀坑相隔百年，但製作於不同時期的假面是如此相似。可以想見，作爲一種宗教藝術，面具的造型必須儼格遵守傳統所規定的模式，不同時期的面具工匠很難有自由發揮的余地。從出土的頭像及姿態各異的人像判斷，當時一定流行戴假面的宗教儀式。戴面具的目的之一是爲了變成假面所表現的神靈。西周時期流行以活人裝扮祖先的祭祀儀式。盡管我們不知當時扮演者（稱作“尸”）是否戴面具，但“尸”與古代三星堆宗教活動中戴面具者的功能是一致的，都是欲與所扮演者合二爲一。戴上表現神靈的面具就變成了那個神靈，因此所有這些戴假面的頭像及人像，既是大型宗教儀式的參與者，又是供人崇拜的偶像。

三星堆面具，很可能與祖先崇拜有關。那幾件縱目面具，或許就是蜀王蠶叢的神化形象。據古史所記早蜀歷史，蠶叢縱目（眼睛外凸），因此稱王。有意思的是，古文字中跟古蜀歷史有關的幾個字，都與眼睛有關。“蜀”在甲骨文中寫作　，由蟲與一雙大眼睛組成。蠶叢，柏灌和魚鳧建都瞿上，漢代的《説文解字》解釋“瞿”爲“鷹隼之視”，乃是一只有一雙巨目的大鳥。盡管縱目面具是否表現蠶叢還值得討論，但古三星堆人的祖先崇拜卻有跡可尋。最明顯的莫過于其對鳥這個形象的偏愛。縱觀三星堆文物，鳥似乎無所不在。它在三星堆藝術中的重要性讓人感到，它可能是當時人圖騰崇拜的產物。古蜀國最早的幾位統治者，柏灌和魚鳧，名字都與水鳥有關。之後的杜宇，或許是爲了證明其改朝換代的正當性，也將名字改成了鳥名，叫做“蒲卑”。考古發掘發現，三星堆二，三期流行一種陶鳥頭柄勺，待到西周初年三星堆古城被廢棄，這種勺也隨之消失。很可能三星堆藝術中流行的勾喙魚鷹形鳥，就是當時人的圖騰物。伴隨鳥出現的是魚的形象。一號坑出土20多件玉璋，刃尖被設計成魚嘴形。同一坑中出土的一根金杖上刻有鳥和中箭的魚的圖形，彷佛是表現涉及魚鷹的捕魚情形。可以想見，刻劃於金杖上的必定是有特殊意味的圖象。另外一件二號坑出土的殘青銅像，表現一個鳥爪人立于兩只鳥頭上。象這樣半人半鳥的形象還出現在同一坑出土的殘大型青銅神壇上，它的重要地位可以由其在那兒的突出位置來判斷。顯然，鳥和人的親密關係導致了鳥的人形化。作爲圖騰物的鳥已突破人與鳥之間的任何藩籬。

盡管解開三星堆祭祀坑之謎還有待時日，但在四川發現一個可與中原媲美的青銅時代，意義非凡。因爲它不僅塡補了我們對古蜀文化瞭解的空白，而且還極大地拓寬了我們對商文明的界定。

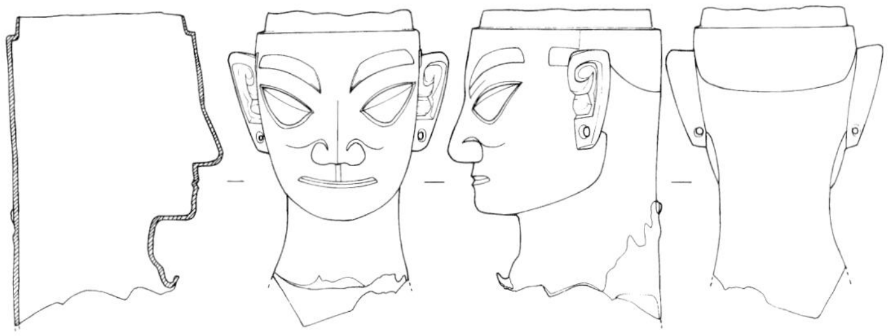

1 Human head
銅人頭像

Middle Shang (c. 1300 BCE)
Bronze
Height 29 cm, width 20.6 cm, weight 4483 g, excavated from Sanxingdui Pit I (K1: 2)
商代中期，高：29 cm 寬：20.6 cm

The most astonishing artefacts from Sanxingdui Pit I are a group of thirteen life-size bronze heads with dramatic facial features. All the heads had been burned and damaged before they were buried in the pit. Among them five images had almost completely melted down leaving only fragments of the top of the head; and the rest were badly damaged on their necks by fire, as is evident in this example.

On comparing the bronze heads from the two pits, what is striking about this one is the rendering of its head which, in terms of the Sanxingdui finds, exhibits a fair degree of realism. With the softer lines to its face and less schematic and uniform features, the head is the only one in the group rendered in this more realistic manner. The humanoid face is immediately identifiable as human and thus poses fewer iconographical problems. While its countenance is expressed realistically, the eyes are treated in an exaggerated way. The almond-shaped eyes are slanting, wide open and characterised by a horizontal ridge across the eyeball.

The flange on the cranium suggests that a separately-cast cap may have crowned the figure. According to archaeologists, the clay core found inside the figure suggests the bronze was made locally, and the foundry was at the Sanxingdui site.

2 Human head
銅人頭像

Middle Shang (c. 1300 BCE)
Bronze
Height 25 cm, width 20.4 cm, weight 3363 g, excavated from Sanxingdui Pit I (K1: 6)
商代中期，高：25 cm 寬：20.4 cm

Unlike the previous head, this image shows strong, rather schematic features. It has slanting, almond-shaped eyes with the eyeball defined by a horizontal ridge. Above the eyes are large brows and below, deep, curved ridges which seem to indicate cheekbones. The comparatively narrow and straight nose and the thin, tightly-defined, upturned mouth are both characteristic features of this type. The ears projecting at right angles to the head are defined by schematic relief, and as with all the bronze heads and masks from Sanxingdui, are pierced at the earlobe for earrings or other ornaments.

The jaw line extends from behind the ear in a sharp right-angled hook which strongly suggests the image is a face mask. The flange on the top of the head reveals two small holes that may have been used to keep a cap or other attachment in position.

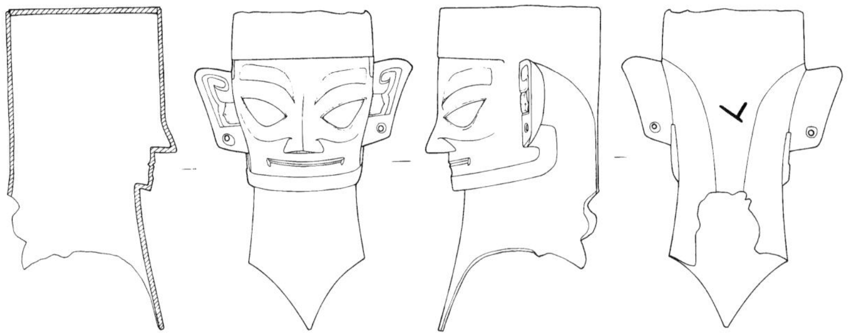

3 Human head with flat cap

銅人頭像

Middle Shang (c. 1300 BCE)
Bronze
Height 37.4 cm, width 26.4 cm, weight 6722 g, excavated from Sanxingdui Pit I (K1: 11)
商代中期，高：37.4 cm 寬：26.4 cm

Nine of the thirteen individual heads found in Pit I wear flat caps such as seen here. All of the heads of this type were designed with pierced ears and hair worn in a pigtail. According to archaeologists, the flat top of the head was cast first, then inserted into the mould of the whole head and secured by the second casting.

While this bronze shares the principal characteristics of the previous image, its head is more compressed. It has a long, strong neck which, as with all the individual heads excavated from the two pits, is cut to a point at the front and back and has been partially damaged by fire. Again, the sharply defined chin that mirrors the horizontal line of the cap gives a mask-like impression.

It was discovered during the excavation that a number of other small objects were contained inside this head including bronze *ge* daggers, gold tiger-like ornaments, jade *zuo* chisels, *yuan* collared rings, and *cong* ritual jades, as well as some cowrie shells.

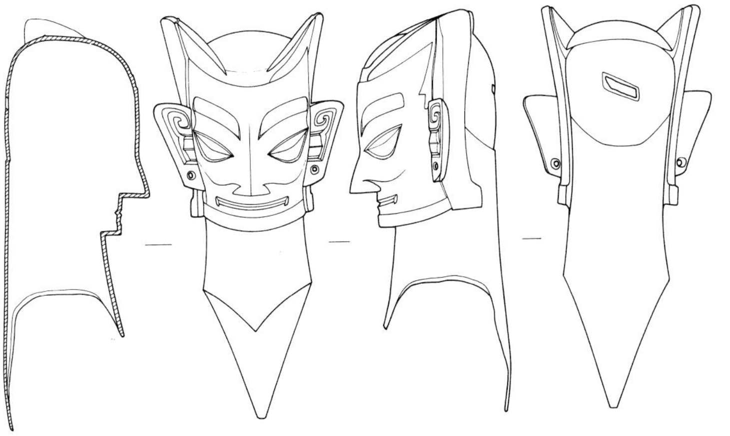

4 Human head
銅人頭像

Middle Shang (c. 1300 BCE)
Bronze
Height 45.6 cm, width 22 cm, weight 4540 g, excavated from Sanxingdui Pit I (K1: 5)
商代中期，高：45.6 cm 寬：22 cm

Basically similar to the preceding head (cat. no. 3) this example is distinguished by its unusual headgear with side protrusions which form part of the overall mask. The 'false face' features a short yet sharp nose and sharp ridges below the eyes. A small hole on the upper part of the back of the head suggests that some sort of ornament was originally inserted here.

The bold features and simple rendering contribute to an impression of resolve and austerity. A stong sense of modernity is generated by the powerful simplicity and definitive geometry of masks like this.

5 Standing figure
銅立人像

Late Shang (c. 1200–1100 BCE)
Bronze
Overall height 260.8 cm, height of figure 180 cm, weight 18000 g, excavated from Sanxingdui Pit II (K2-2: 149)
商代晚期，通高：260.8 cm 人高：180 cm

As the only complete example of a large-scale human sculpture in bronze known to us from the Shang (c. 1600–1100 BCE) and Western Zhou dynasties (c. 1100–771 BCE), this would have to be the most remarkable statue of China's Bronze Age. Standing barefoot upon a base the figure wears a crown consisting of a headband with incised paired-loop motifs topped by a headdress which flares outwards and is decorated with intaglio lines. The face of the figure shares the features of many of the bronze heads discovered in the two pits which again suggest a mask. He wears a leg band on each ankle and three bracelets on each arm. Most striking of all is the position of the arms and the oversized, cupped hands which clearly indicate that they were originally made to hold an object, but it is not clear what this might have been. Archaeologists suggest either a jade *cong*, an item important to ritual activity, or an elephant tusk. The exaggerated circumference of the hands and the angle of their hollowed grip suggest they held a massive and curved object.

The figure wears a garment of three layers. The outer garment leaves the left shoulder free and ends in a short sleeve on the right. The motifs on the left side beneath the raised arm are pairs of schematic dragons clearly designed in such a way as to echo the ubiquitous *taotie* mask. The two vertical borders are ornamented with bands of scroll motifs on the inner border, and stylised animal heads with large eyes and three-pointed crowns on the outer border. A ribbon runs across the chest from the right shoulder to form two knots at the back. The middle garment has short sleeves and folds across the front, forcing a deep V-shaped opening over the chest and the back, but is otherwise barely visible. The undergarment, which ends in the sweeping tails at the back of the figure, is principally visible on the lower portion of the figure. It is decorated with variations of the *taotie* or dragon motif, dominated by large eyes and scroll patterns. Beneath are larger versions of the animal mask with a three-pointed crown. All these decorative devices and patterns reflect the symbolic style and aesthetic of the decor on Shang ritual bronze vessels. The complexity in style and decoration of the garment indicate the high status of the figure. The elaborate costume also suggests that a textile industry was well developed in the ancient Shu kingdom. This is supported by a number of spindle whorls excavated at the Sanxingdui site which would have been used in conjunction with hand spindles and distaffs to make yarns.

The figure stands upon a flat platform decorated on four sides with geometric patterns. Supporting this platform are four elephant-like heads on each corner of the square base. When inverted their design bears a strong resemblance to the *taotie* mask. Each of the animals' heads has a pair of slanting, exaggerated eyes, a trunk and tusk curled up at the end, and exposed teeth. Their upturned ears form the four legs that support the platform above. A further square base with a plain surface below raises the figure to an imposing position.

According to archaeologists, the figure had been smashed into several pieces before it was buried, and the clay found inside the figure is the original casting core. A close examination reveals that the figure was first made in separate pieces, such as head, torso and limbs, and then assembled through a second casting.

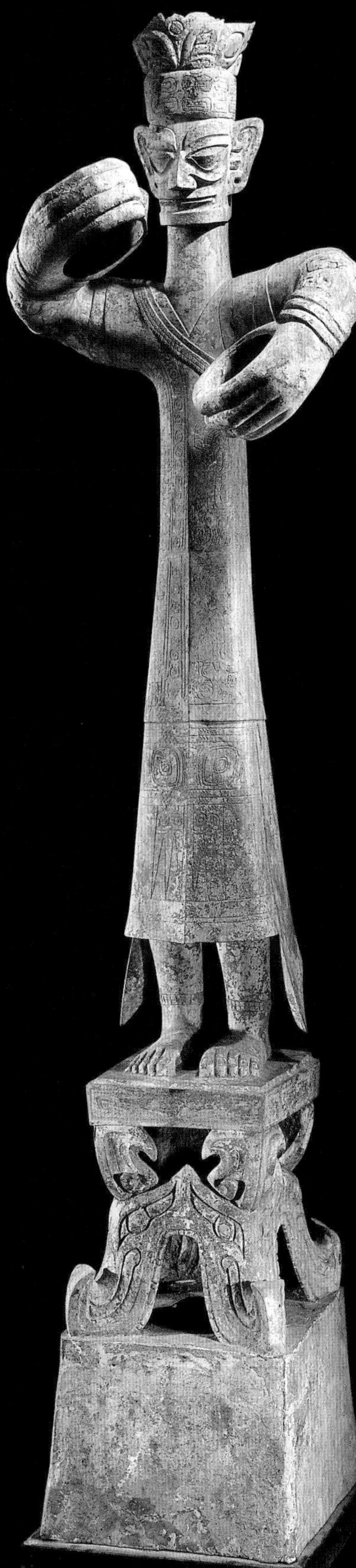

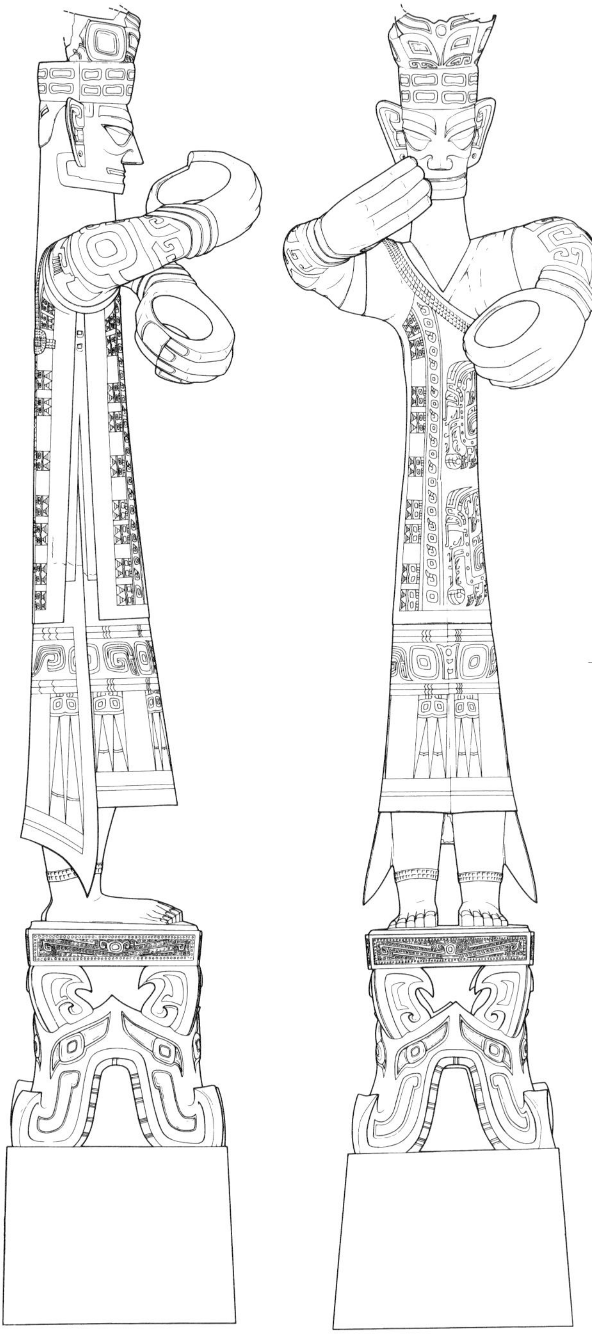

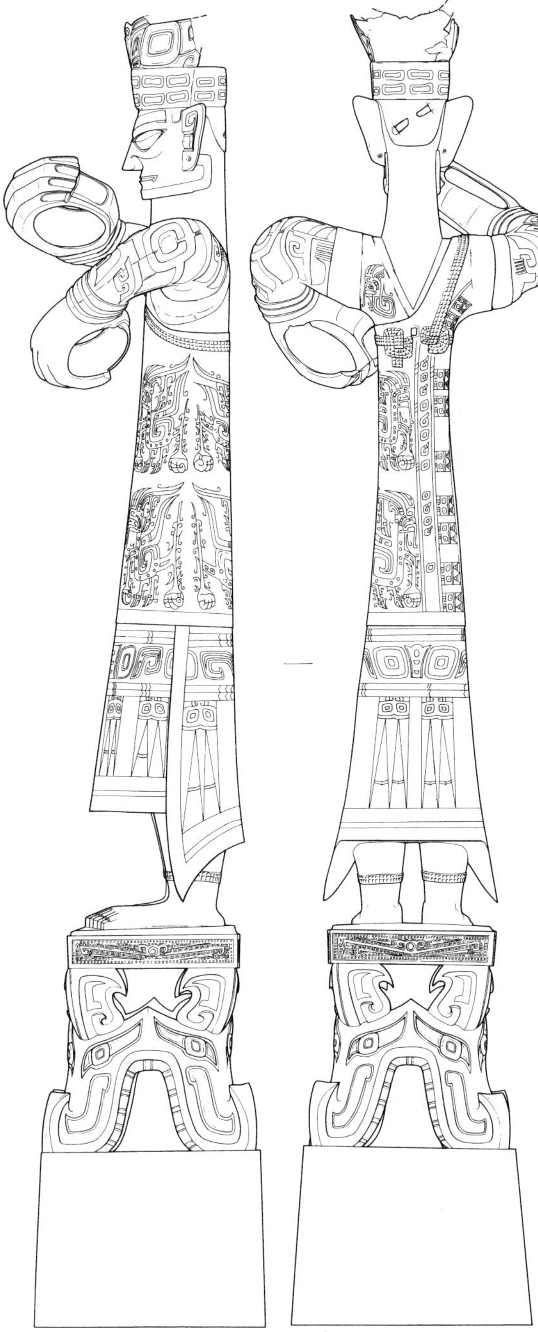

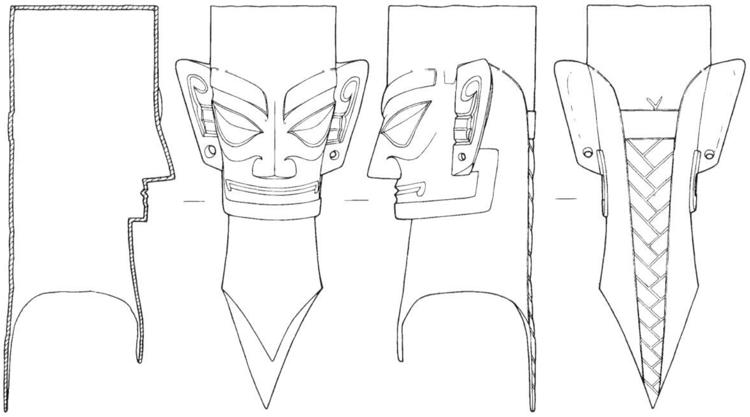

6 Human head with flat top
銅人頭像

Late Shang (c. 1200–1100 BCE)
Bronze
Height 40.4 cm, width 20 cm, weight 4200 g, excavated from Sanxingdui Pit II (K2-2: 51)
商代晚期，高：40.4 cm 寬：20 cm

Of the total group of forty-four individual bronze heads discovered in Pit II, thirty-six share facial features similar to this image. The features of the predominant head type are very like those of the free-standing figure. These include an elongated face, large slanting eyes, heavy rough brows and sharply defined cheek-bones, and a thin-lipped mouth which is broader than those on images found in Pit I. The ears project at right angles to the head and are pierced at the bottom. Traces of black pigment are found on the eye sockets and hair and vermilion on the nostrils and mouth. A long plait draped down the back of the head is tied at the upper section. The pierced ears and hair fastened in a pigtail are features similar to other bronze heads from Pit I. A sharp right-angled hook bending back behind the ears strongly suggests the frame of a mask.

Research indicates two methods were involved in the casting of these images. In most of the cases, the flat top of the head was cast first and then inserted into the mould of the whole head and secured by the second casting (as mentioned in cat. no. 3). In some other cases, a hole about 6–7 cm wide was reserved during the first cast and filled in the second cast.

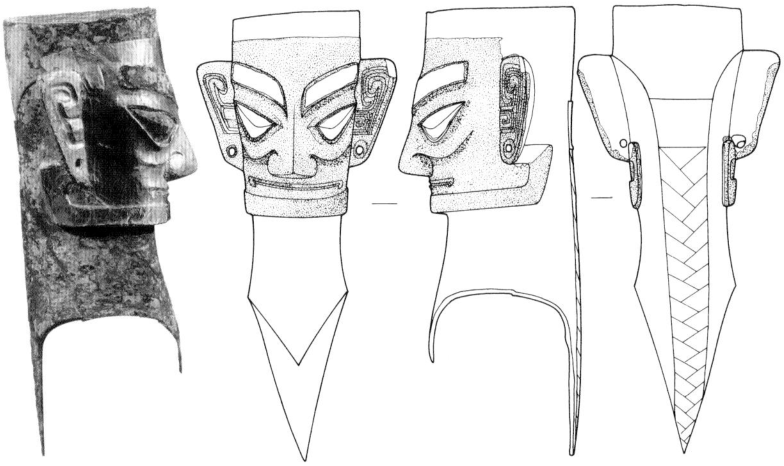

7 Head with gold leaf
金面銅人頭像

Late Shang (c. 1200–1100 BCE)
Bronze
Height 42.5 cm, width 19.6 cm, weight 2550 g, excavated from Sanxingdui Pit II (K2-2: 45)
商代晚期，高：42.5 cm 寬：19.6 cm

This is one of four bronze heads from Pit II where the face is covered with applied gold leaf. Two of these four have flat craniums, one of which is included here, and the other two have round heads decorated with headgear. The face and ears of this head are covered completely with gold leaf, leaving exposed only the large slanting eyes, brows, and earring-holes. According to archaeologists, the beaten gold foil was attached to the face with an adhesive made of resin. As on the other pieces, the head seems to be disguised by a mask. Seen from the rear, the figure has a flat-topped cap from which falls a long plait.

Other gold artefacts excavated from both pits include ornaments of gold foil and roughly life-sized masks hammered from gold sheet which, unfortunately, cannot be matched with any of the bronze heads.

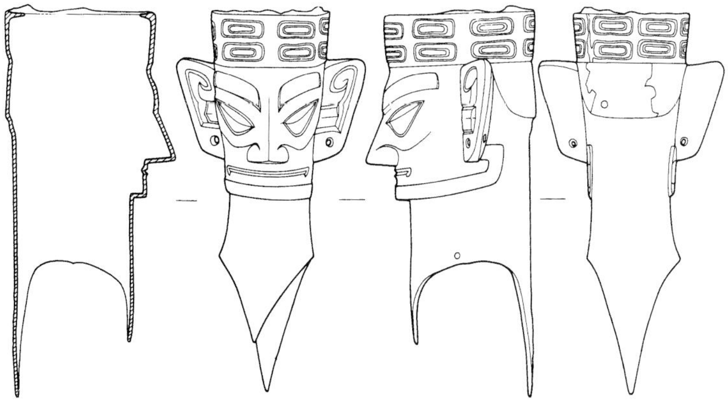

8 Human head with flat cap
銅人頭像

Late Shang (c. 1200–1100 BCE)
Bronze
Height 34.8 cm, width 17.2 cm, weight 2081 g, excavated from Sanxingdui Pit II (K2-2: 90)
商代晚期，高：34.8 cm 寬：17.2 cm

This figure is in a category of its own because of its flat-topped cap decorated with intaglio motifs. The motifs resemble those on the lower section of the crown worn by the large standing figure (cat. no. 5) and which bear a resemblance to the 'broad figure band' motif on later Western Zhou bronze vessels. Besides this feature, the bronze is typical of the heads found in Pit II with strongly slanting eyes, high cheekbones, a wide, upturned mouth, and a pair of ears projecting at right angles to the head. The small holes on the neck may offer a clue as to how these heads were fixed on bodies that have been made of less precious materials. All the heads have relatively long necks which are cut to points in the front and back. The acute angled, pen nib-like necks puzzled the archaeologists who at first considered that these heads might have originally been installed on huge wooden columns. However, from the triangular neck opening on the garment of the free-standing figure – which perfectly matches the shape of the pointed neck – Chinese archaeologists have further suggested that the heads were probably mounted on supports of some other material such as wood or clay.

It has also been suggested that the top part of the cap, now missing, and the rest of the head were cast separately and were then joined together through a second casting operation.

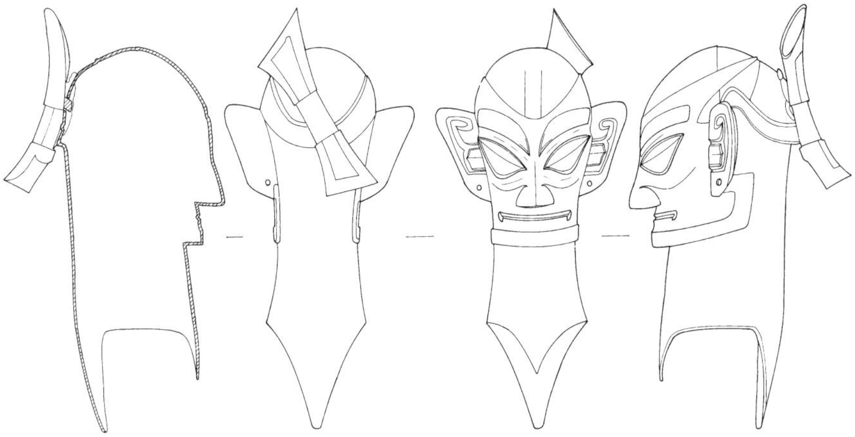

9 Human head with a headgear
銅人頭像

Late Shang (c. 1200–1100 BCE)
Bronze
Overall height 51.6 cm, width 23.8 cm, weight 5800 g, excavated from Sanxingdui Pit II (K2-2: 58)
商代晚期，高：51.6 cm 寬：23.8 cm

The head has angular facial features tapered slightly below, a pair of enormous slanting eyes, a short nose defined by curved ridges and a broad, thin-lipped mouth. Traces of black and vermilion are clearly seen on the brows, eye sockets, nostrils, mouth and earring-holes. A flange which projects slightly around the rear of the head suggests that the figure may wear a close-fitting cap; headgear in the shape of an angled bow tie is designed as an additional section which is attached at the back of the head. It seems to have been cast first and then inserted into the mould for the whole head, thus fixed into position by the second casting. The curved line which extends from the forehead toward the rear of the head, and the sharp right-angled hook behind the ears again gives a strong impression that the face is actually covered by a mask. Three other heads found in Pit II share an almost identical pattern with this one. Two of them, however, have applied gold foil covering their faces.

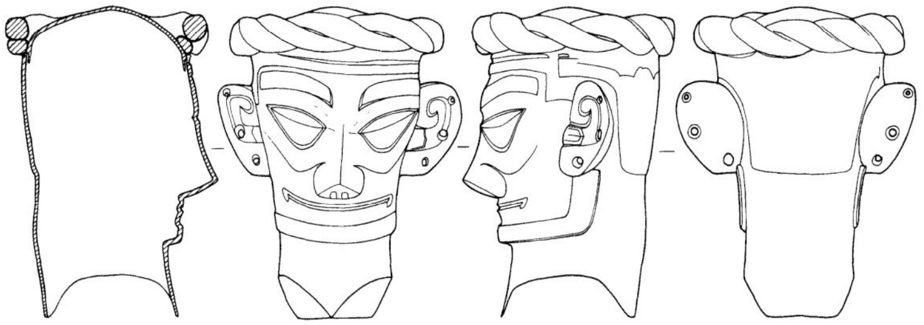

10 Human head with a rolled turban
銅人頭像

Late Shang (c. 1200–1100 BCE)
Bronze
Height 13.6 cm, width 10.8 cm, weight 710 g, excavated from Sanxingdui Pit II (K2-2: 83)
商代晚期，高：13.6 cm 寬：10.8 cm

This is the only example of a turbaned head among all the bronze heads from Sanxingdui pits. The image shares the principal facial features of the predominant type of head, however, it is smaller in scale, and the face is more elegantly tapered towards the chin. The headdress is unique too – on the round head with short hair there sits a rolled turban. Compared to other heads, the ears and the nose are treated in softer lines and appear more realistic. Three small holes are seen in each of the ears.

11 Human mask
銅人面具

Middle Shang (c. 1300 BCE)
Bronze
Height 7 cm, width 9.2 cm, thickness 0.4 cm, weight 145 g, excavated from Sanxingdui Pit I (K1: 20)
商代中期，高：7 cm 寬：9.2 cm

Masks found at Sanxingdui range in style from comparatively realistic to purely symbolic types: while some are close to portraits, others resemble more schematic forms of human image. This is one of the two masks found in Pit I. It is unique and very different from the majority of human masks discovered in Sanxingdui pits, not only in scale but also in the crudely executed treatment of the surface, and in its facial features. The figure has sharp ridges below the eye sockets but otherwise displays normal human features. The ears are indistinct and pierced at the bottom. One other human mask from Pit I (K1: 4), 14.9 cm high, was badly damaged. It, however, displays facial features similar to those found in Pit II.

12 Human mask
銅人面具

Late Shang (c. 1200–1100 BCE)
Bronze
Height 40.3 cm, width 60.5 cm, thickness 0.6 cm, weight 13400 g, excavated from Sanxingdui Pit II (K2-2: 153)
商代晚期，高：40.3 cm 寬：60.5 cm

Although fragments found in Pit II suggest that larger masks of up to 120 centimetres wide and 80 centimetres high could have existed, this image was the largest intact mask of its type. A group of twenty masks of the same type from Pit II are characterised by a U-shaped structure when viewed from above. The large slanting eyes framed by bold outlines, strongly curled nostrils and very broad tight-lipped mouth give the image a surreal dimension. The sharp right-angled hook which bends back behind the ears, extending the line of the jaw, further confirms the impression observed in previous individual heads – they were all disguised by masks. Like the bronze heads, the ears of this mask are pierced for earrings. Traces of vermilion are still visible on the mouth.

On each side of the mask, three small holes are seen above and below the ears, as well as at the end of the brows. These holes suggest that the mask must have been attached to a sculpture of some other material. Close examination led archaeologists to conclude that the mask was completed in one casting operation.

13 Human mask
銅人面具

Late Shang (c. 1200–1100 BCE)
Bronze
Height 25.5 cm, width 42.5 cm, thickness 0.3 cm, weight 3400 g, excavated from Sanxingdui Pit II (K2-2: 33)
商代晚期，高：25.5 cm 寬：42.5 cm

Of the twenty masks with human-like features the majority are large in scale and are all broadly in a horizontal as opposed to vertical format. It shares with the previous mask the dominant feature of a pair of slanting eyes characterised by a horizontal ridge across the eyeball. The sharp ridge below the eye socket enhances the tapered cheek. The square hole on the forehead was chiselled out by a sharp tool later. A different casting method was also observed with this piece: it is thought that the ears and the main face of the mask were cast separately and joined together through a second operation.

14 Human mask

銅人面具

Late Shang (c. 1200–1100 BCE)
Bronze
Height 15.4 cm, width 18.2 cm, thickness 0.3 cm, weight 1090 g, excavated from Sanxingdui Pit II (K2-2: 331)
商代晚期，高：15.4 cm 寬：18.2 cm

Though it shares the primary features of the majority of masks, this image along with six other pieces found in Pit II represents a slightly different model. These masks are much smaller and higher than they are wide. On this mask, apart from the pierced ears, another four small holes are seen on the chin and on the corners below the ears. There are traces of black pigment on brows, eyeballs and eye sockets.

Like the individual heads, these masks possess certain human characteristics which are expressed through the witty exaggeration of facial features. However, these features are abstracted, distancing them from reality and giving the mask its formal and inherently symbolic characteristics.

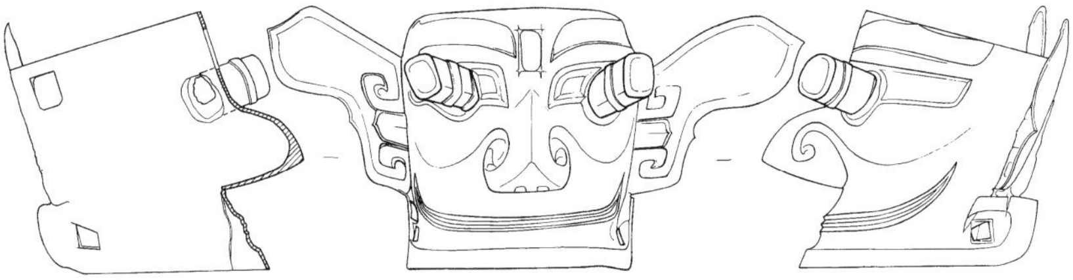

15 Zoomorphic human mask with protruding pupils
銅獸面具

Late Shang (c. 1200–1100 BCE)
Bronze
Height 66 cm, width 138 cm, excavated from Sanxingdui Pit II (K2-2: 148)
商代晚期，高：66 cm 寬：138 cm

Among the most striking of all Sanxingdui masks are the examples illustrated here and in the next entry. This is the largest of three grotesque masks found at Pit II. It shares some facial features of bronze heads and masks previously mentioned such as the deep sunken grooves below the eyes indicating cheekbones. However, animal forms are freely combined with human features in this work. This mask has an exceptionally broad mouth with a tongue – showing between tightly pursed lips. The chin protrudes sharply and the nose in profile is determined by a bold curving line with nostrils marked by emphatic curls. The enormous projecting ears drawn to sharp tips, and a pair of long, slanting eyes from which protrude cylinder-shaped pupils with a band at the centre (16.5 cm long, 13.5 cm in diameter) are like those in other examples of these extraordinary masks. Forms such as this exude a sense of superhuman power. The ears, nose, and mouth evoke a strange, bestial quality whilst its otherworldly eyes are frightening to behold.

Two square holes on either side of this mask suggest it may have been attached to a body of other material. It is possible that the square hole on the forehead may have been used to fit an ornamental projection like the one visible in cat. no. 16. Close observation reveals that these holes were chiselled out later when the mask had been in use for sometime. According to archaeologists, the protruding pupils, the ears and the other parts of the mask were cast individually and then embedded in the mould for a second cast to fuse them together.

16 Zoomorphic human mask with ornamented forehead and protruding pupils
銅獸面具

Late Shang (c. 1200–1100 BCE)
Bronze
Overall height 82.5, mask height 31.5 cm, width 77.4 cm, weight 1700 g, excavated from Sanxingdui Pit II (K2-2: 142)
商代晚期，高：82.5 cm 寬：31.5 cm

The overall pattern of this mask is similar to the giant mask in the previous entry, but there are subtle differences between them in individual details. They both have a pair of enormous ears, for instance, but in this example they project horizontally rather than upward. This mask also shows the characteristic ridged eyelids decorated with black pigment. Traces of the black pigment are also seen on the brows, and vermilion pigment is evident on the broad, tight-lipped mouth. A pair of bulging eyes protruding like cylinders and a long projection rising upward from the nose (68 cm high) create a sense of the supernatural. This projection coils at the top and bottom, and has a cusped, knife-shaped section in between. This motif, which the archaeologists have termed *kuilong* or 'hornless dragon', is one of the most prevalent decorative patterns seen in the artefacts discovered in Sanxingdui pits. It also occurs, for instance, on the clothes of the standing figure (cat. no. 5), on the ornamental projections of the bronze snakes (cat. no. 28), and even on the small bands of relief suggesting the hollows of the ears of the heads and masks, as well as on the leg 'tattoos' of a semi-human figure (cat. no. 23). The close resemblance of such motifs to those seen on the bronzes from the metropolitan Shang area and elsewhere provides strong evidence of a degree of contact between Sanxingdui and the other parts of China.

Two square holes in both sides of the mask may have functioned to attach it to a body of other material.

17 Animal mask
銅獸面具

Late Shang (c. 1200–1100 BCE)
Bronze
Height 20.8 cm, width 26.9 cm, thickness 0.2 cm, weight 345 g, excavated from Sanxingdui Pit II (K2-3: 230)
商代晚期，高：20.8 cm 寬：26.9 cm

Nine bronze masks of animal faces were discovered in Pit II. They are all plain on the back. The great round eyes, geometric headdress, and wide mouth are particularly prominent features, and remains of black pigment are visible on the eyes, forehead and mouth in many masks. Several small holes on each mask suggest that they may have been fitted to some other object. The nine animal masks may be categorised into three types with three examples in each category: this represents the first type. It appears to have coiled horns arising from the brows, and ornaments on the top of the head. Dominating the face is the pair of round and slightly bulging eyes with pupils outlined in black pigment. The nose is narrow and straight, and has a sharp central ridge; the mouth opens widely exposing the teeth, and the schematic ears which are variations of the ornaments on the head, have incised, curved lines indicating hollows. Below the jaw is a pair of eye-like forms, rising to sharp tips with the corners turned down at the centre. There are four small holes on top of the head and on the jaw respectively.

18 Animal mask
銅獸面具

Late Shang (c. 1200–1100 BCE)
Bronze
Height 21.6 cm, width 39 cm, thickness 0.2 cm, weight 545g, excavated from Sanxingdui Pit II (K2-3: 228)
商代晚期，高：21.6 cm 寬：39 cm

This is the largest example of the group of animal masks and represents the second type. It is a simplified form of the first type: it does not have a pair of eye-like forms below the jaw but otherwise shares the primary features of the previous example.

Aggressive supernatural spirits of an almost demonic nature are represented by these masks. They remind us of the *taotie* animal face – the prevalent motif on ritual objects in Bronze Age China and which is also employed as decoration on bronze vessels in Sanxingdui (see p. 38, fig. 9).

19 Animal mask
铜獸面具

Late Shang (c. 1200–1100 BCE)
Bronze
Height 12.3 cm, width 27.8 cm, thickness 0.2 cm, weight 234 g, excavated from Sanxingdui Pit II (K2-3: 231-1)
商代晚期，高：12.3 cm 寬：27.8 cm

This mask is an example of the third category of animal mask, which displays a further simplification of the first type. The eyes are placed higher joining the eyebrows; the ears are completely omitted, and the teeth are drawn in. Noticeably, black pigment was used to paint pupils and decoration on the head ornaments.

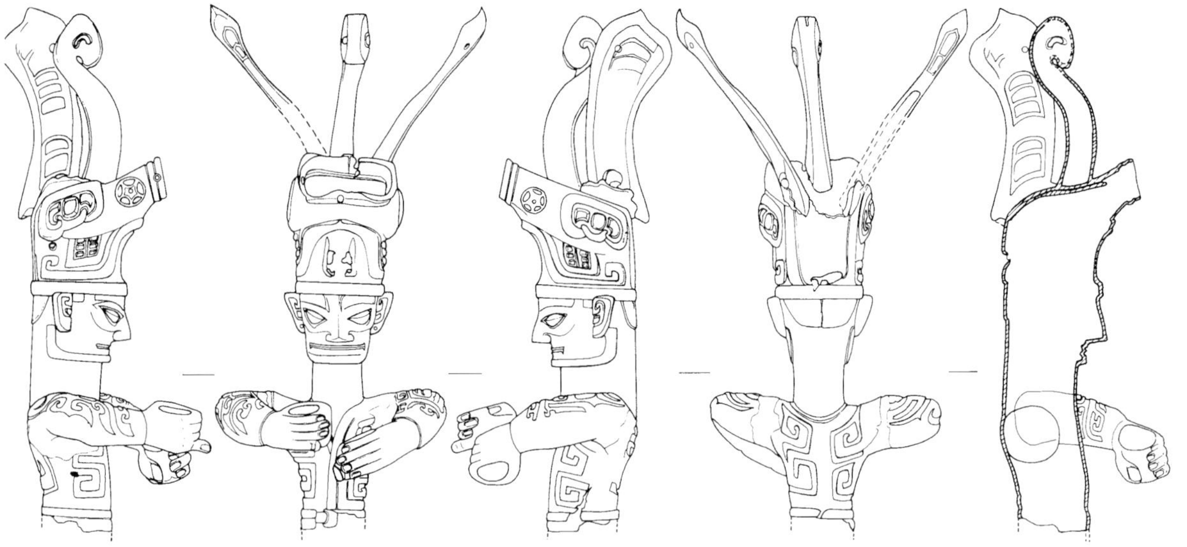

20 Figure with animal headdress
銅獸首冠人像

Late Shang (c. 1200–1100 BCE)
Bronze
Height 40.2 cm, width 18.4 cm, weight 3046 g, excavated from Sanxingdui Pit II (K2-3: 264)
商代晚期，高：40.2 cm 寬：18.4 cm

Besides the large life-size figure (cat. no. 5), Pit II also yielded several other quasi-human statues. They are much smaller in scale campared with the large figure, yet share the same posture with coiled arms and cupped hands that suggest they were intended to hold something. In this example, only the upper part of the body has survived. The figure is clad with a robe folded in front and kept in position by a girdle. The robe is decorated with a meander motif on the front and the back, and a schematic dragon-pattern on the sleeves – both popular motifs on Shang bronze vessels. The severe features of what is probably a mask on the figure and the strong, column-like neck have the same quality as the individual heads. Dominating the figure is what archaeologists have termed an 'animal-like headdress', which forms a trapezium shape when viewed from the side. It has an eye on each side, a big, rectangular 'mouth' opening to the front, a pair of elongated ears (16 cm long) and an ornament in the shape of an elephant's trunk projecting from the top. The use of the term 'animal-like' to describe the headdress is easier to discern when one compares it with the animal figure supporting the fragment of an altar (see p. 26, fig. 3).

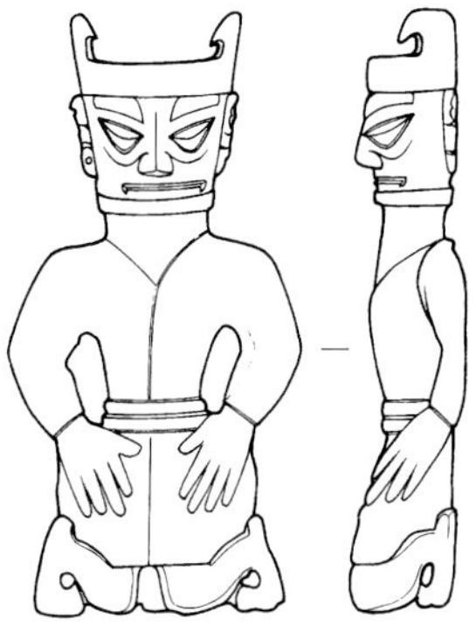

21 Kneeling figure
銅跪坐人像

Late Shang (c. 1200–1100 BCE)
Bronze
Height 12.4 cm, width 5.8 cm, weight 70 g, excavated from Sanxingdui Pit II (K2-3: 05)
商代晚期，高：12.4 cm 寬：5.8 cm

This figure is one of three kneeling figures excavated in Pit II. The figure is seated *en face* with his legs tucked beneath him (*guizuo* in Chinese) and his hands resting on his thighs. This posture was considered quite common in the aristocratic society of the Shang dynasty, being an appropriate position for ritual activities and for receiving guests in a polite manner.[1] It is uncertain whether or not the Sanxingdui people shared the same custom.

The figure wears a mask that is kept in position by a cap-like band with horn-like projections on the side. On other figures of this type small holes are present in the bodies, but not in this example.

1. Li Ji, 'Guizuo, dunji yu qiju' (On the postures of *guizuo*, *dunji* and *qiju*), *Journal of the Institute of History and Philology Academia Sinica*, Taibei, 24 (1953): 283–301.

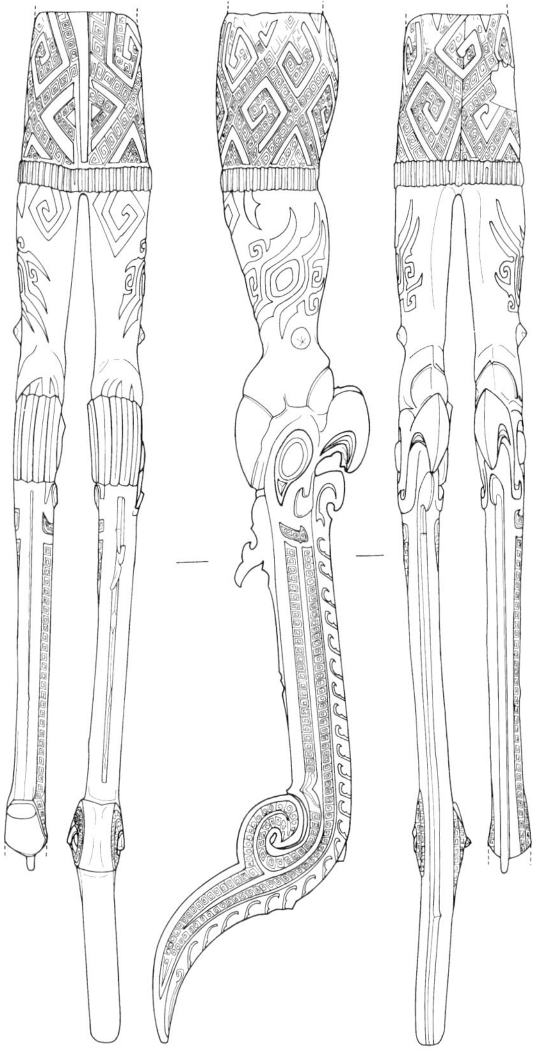

22 Semi-human figure
銅鳥爪人像

Late Shang (c. 1200–1100 BCE)
Bronze
Overall height 81.4 cm, width 10.8 cm, human-like figure height 30 cm, excavated from Sanxingdui Pit II. (K2-3: 327)
商代晚期，高：81.4 cm 寬：10.8 cm

To the fantastic array of Sanxingdui bronzes can be added this figure with a human body and bird's feet. Preserved only in fragmentary form, it is made up of two parts: a human body with bird's feet on the top and two birds below. Archaeological evidence indicates the two parts were joined together through a second cast. The human-bird figure appears to wear a luxuriously decorated, short skirt trimmed with a fringe. Care was taken to enrich the skirt with detail. The decorative patterns here are broad meanders set off by a ground pattern of dense, finely carved spirals. Such motifs are reminiscent of those seen frequently on Shang bronze vessels and testify to a strong influence from the metropolitan Shang area. The geometric patterns employed to ornament the two legs may indicate actual tattoos. Beneath the figure's talons is the pair of richly decorated, stylised and elongated bird forms. With bulging eyes, hooked beaks, elongated necks, and simplified bodies, these are birds of fantasy in concept but ritualistic in flavour.

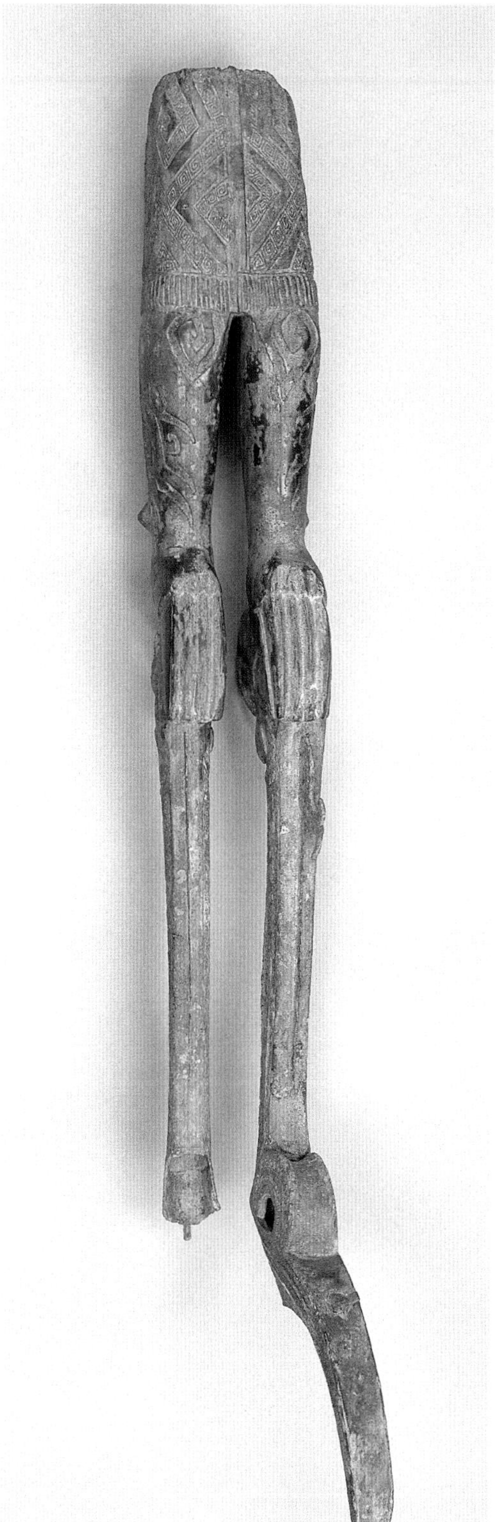

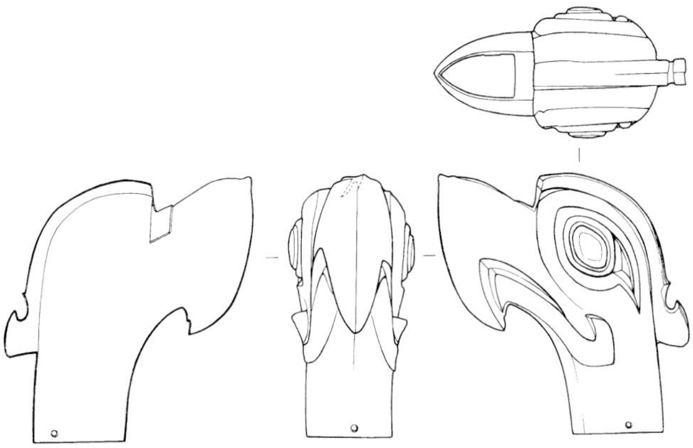

23 Bird's head
銅鳥頭

Late Shang (c. 1200–1100 BCE)
Bronze
Height 40.3 cm, width 38.8 cm, excavated from Sanxingdui Pit II (K2-2: 141)
商代晚期，高：40.3 cm 寬：38.8 cm

The dominant features of this bird's head are its pronounced, hooked beak, and a pair of enormous eyes encircled by a steeply sloping frame giving it the overall impression of a bird of prey, perhaps an eagle. The eyelids and beak of the bird were decorated originally with vermilion. Three small holes on the bottom of the neck suggest that it may have been part of a large figure.

As an object the head is characterised by its powerful sculptural quality which is an unusual feature in the tentative realism of Shang art. It is an image of elegant simplicity in which the sparse use of lines to depict the features of the head conveys a palpable sensation of immediacy and presence. It is an object of antiquity imbued with a credible modernity.

Fig. 1. The fragment of a large bronze tree, late Shang (c. 1200–1100 BCE), height 142 cm; excavated from Sanxingdui Pit II (K2-2: 194).

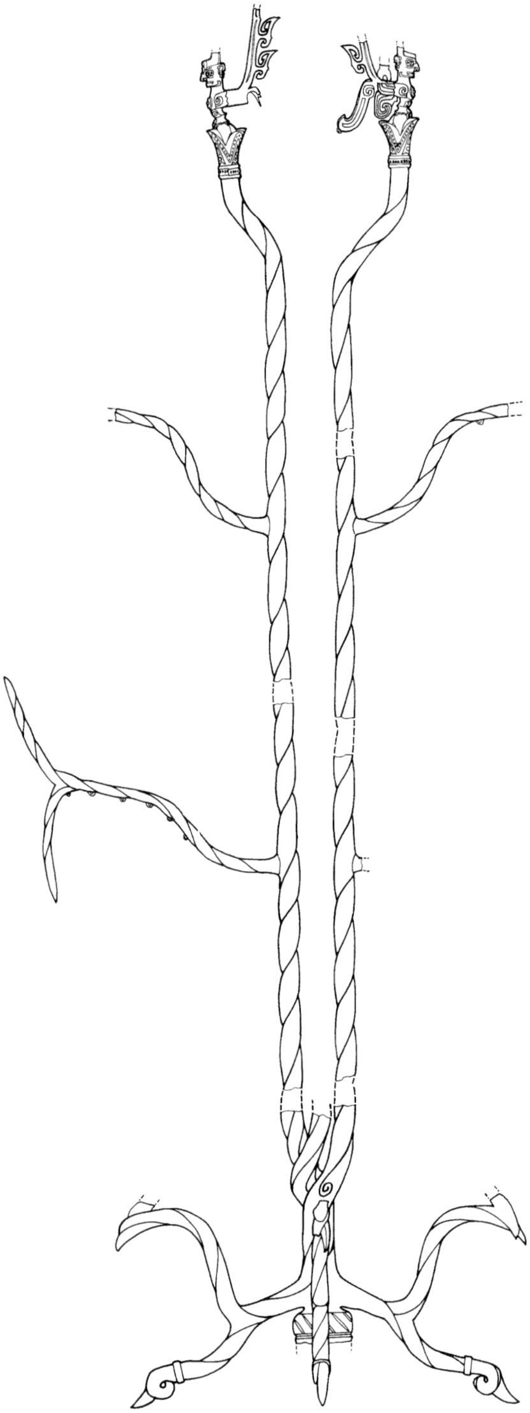

Fig. 2. Drawing of a bronze tree, late Shang (c. 1200–1100 BCE), height 50 cm; excavated from Sanxingdui Pit II (K2-3: 272).

24 Human-head bird finial
銅人首鳥身像

Late Shang (c. 1200–1100 BCE)
Bronze
Height 12 cm, excavated from Sanxingdui Pit II (K2-3: 154)

商代晚期，高：12 cm

Several bronze trees decorated with birds and fruits were discovered in Pit II. The archaeologists have so far pieced together three bronze trees from broken and charred remains (see p. 25, fig. 1; p. 90, figs 1–2). These vary in height from approximately 50 cm to 396 cm, and all have gracefully curving branches emerging from the trunk supporting leaves and fruits. The elaborate construction of the bronze trees with numerous pendants and ornaments indicates that they must have played an important role in the ceremonial and religious activities of the people of the area. Some of the fruit finials were even covered with gold leaf on their branches.

This tiny figure belonged to a small bronze tree that originally comprised three straight, rope-like trunks, but only two of them have been reconstructed (see opposite, fig. 2). Each of the two surviving branches bears a flower bud on its end upon which perches a hybrid bird. The fantastic creature is a combination of human and bird elements. It has a crowned head wearing a human-like mask. The crown is similar to the one worn by the kneeling figure (cat. no. 21) and consists of large upward bands which are also probably part of the mask. The bird-like body has a full breast decorated with scrolls and outstretched wings. The similar human-headed bird also appeared on a large altar fragment in bronze (see p. 26, fig. 3).

25 Bird finial
銅花蕾小鳥

Late Shang (c. 1200–1100 BCE)
Bronze
Height 7.8 cm; width 4.3 cm; weight 37 g;
excavated from Sanxingdui Pit II (K2-2: 47)
商代晚期，高：7.8 cm 寬：4.3 cm

Along with other pendants and ornaments in the form of flowers and fruits, this bird was used to decorate one of the bronze trees found in Pit II. Perching upon a flower bud, displaying its erect crest and outstretched tail feathers, the bird is a striking combination of realism and imagination. Figure eight-shaped bronze rings are still attached to its tail.

Birds were a favoured subject in Sanxingdui bronze art. Indeed, the extreme popularity of the bird motif leads to the suggestion that birds may have played an important role in the ceremonial and religious worlds of the ancient Sanxingdui inhabitants, and that the motif could have been used by the people of the area as some kind of clan emblem.

26 Bird
銅鳥

Late Shang (c. 1200–1100 BCE)
Bronze
Height 27.8 cm, width 15.4 cm; weight 987 g; excavated from Sanxingdui Pit II (K2-3: 301-3)
商代晚期，高：27.8 cm 寬：15.4 cm

Besides those that appear to belong to bronze trees, a number of bronze birds on a slightly larger scale such as this one also came to light in Pit II. The base is hollow with four small holes at the narrow waist indicating that the bird must have been attached as a finial. A small hole on its beak suggests that originally it had a ring attached. Although its crest and tail are missing, the bird still exhibits a vivid, fantastic quality.

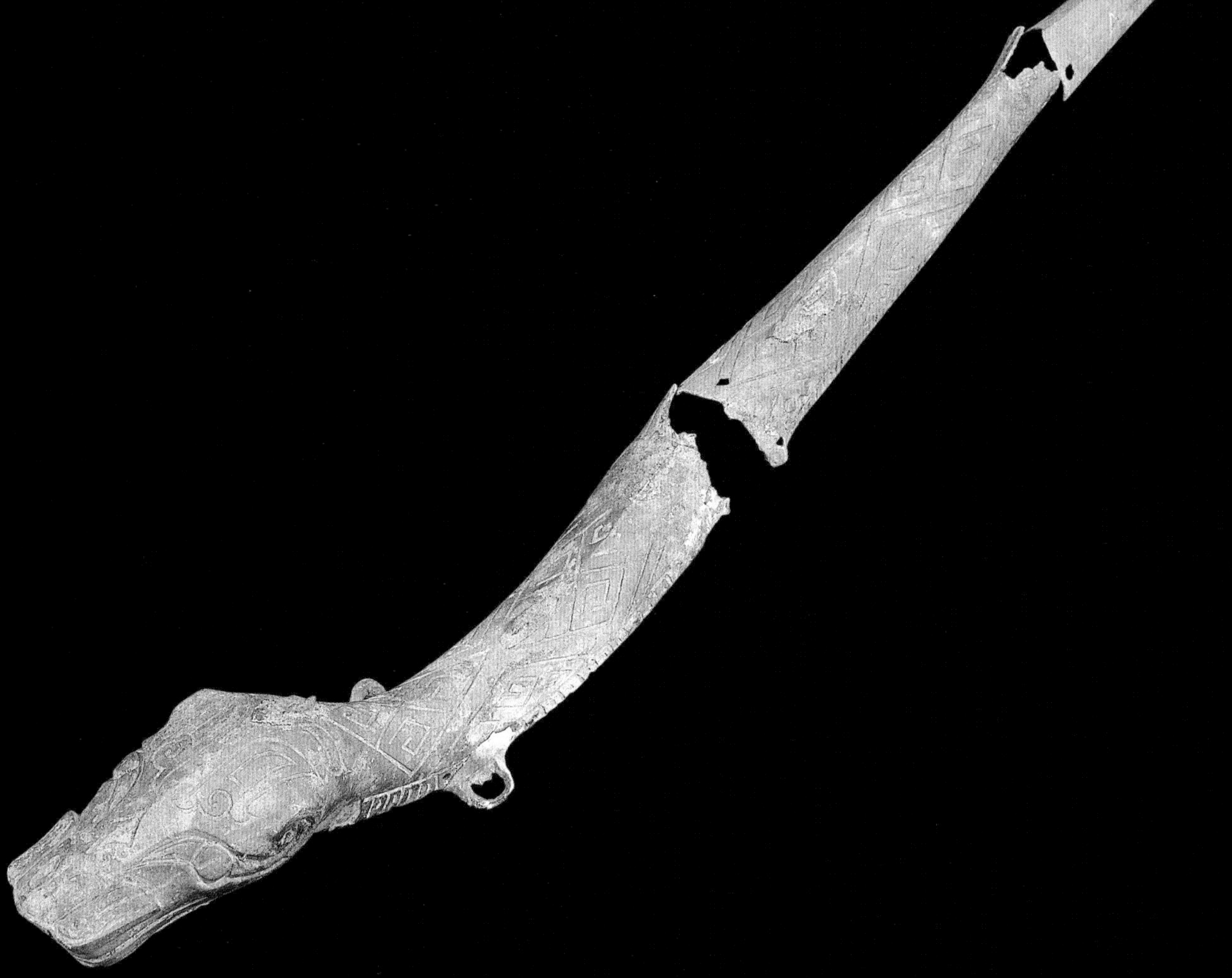

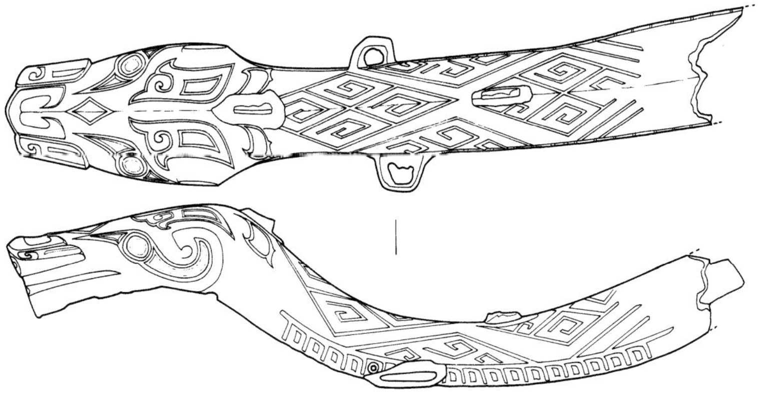

27 Snake

銅蛇

Late Shang (c. 1200–1100 BCE)
Bronze
Length 110.5 cm; width 5-10 cm; weight 4218 g; excavated from Sanxingdui Pit II (K2-3: 87, K2-3: 56, K2-2: 44)
商代晚期，高：110.5 cm 寬：5-10 cm

From fragments discovered in Pit II, archaeologists have pieced together two bronze snakes. They appear to be in three sections, each cast separately and jointed together through a second casting operation. With its head raised up and tail curved inward, this piece displays the movement of a living creature. The primary decorative pattern on its body is the continuous geometric lozenge-shaped design bordered by an incised meander. Three knife-shaped projections were originally fitted on its head, neck and back. There are two rings attached to the sides of its neck.

28 Fitting in form of a wheel
銅太陽形器

Late Shang (c. 1200–1100 BCE)
Bronze
Diameter 85 cm; weight 6000 g; excavated from Sanxingdui Pit II (K2-2: 67)
商代晚期，直徑：85 cm

Six or so wheel-shaped objects have been reconstructed from fragments found in Pit II. Each of these 'wheels' has a round, almost bulbous centre, from which emerge five spokes. A close examination reveals that the centre, the spokes and the outside ring were cast individually and fabricated through a second casting.

These bronzes are among the most enigmatic objects discovered in the Sanxingdui pits. The question as to the function of the wheels remains unanswered. One suggestion is that they could be chariot wheels, yet it is difficult to imagine why they are all hollow at the back and relatively thin, or why the pits yielded nothing else related to the chariot. Archaeologists have excavated a number of chariot wheels in the Shang capital Anyang.[1] These wheels were all made of wood with bronze mountings. The scale of these wheels generally ranged from 120–140 cm in diameter with 18 or more spokes. More significantly, the excavated carriage wheels all have an open nave boss through which the axle was fixed. All these characteristics are quite different from the Sanxingdui examples. Another suggestion is that the bronze was an ornament attached to some other object, a wooden shield for instance. Bronze mountings of wooden shields in a similar form were found from the early Western Zhou tombs in a neighbouring area of the Shu kingdom in Baoji, Shaanxi province where the Sanxingdui influence was obvious.[2] In one other attempt to explain the wheels, some scholars have speculated that they may represent the sun with the spokes representing the sun's rays. Their hypothesis was based on rock paintings with similar motifs found in Gongxian in Sichuan, Huashan at Ningming, in Guangxi and Changyuan in Yunnan. They believed that, as in many cults of ancient civilisations, the sun might have played a special role in the belief of Sanxingdui inhabitants. Although the plausibility of these interpretations is still in question, one thing is almost certain: the small holes on the outside ring and the bulbous centre of the bronze mean that the 'wheel' had been mounted on some other object.

1. Anyang Excavation Team '*Anyang Yixu xiaomingtun de liangzuo chemakeng*' (Two carriage-horse pits at Xiaomingtun in Anyang), *Kaogu*, 1 (1977): 69–70; and '*Anyang xing faxian de Yindai chemakeng*' (The newly discovered carriage-horse pit at Anyang), *Kaogu*, 6 (1984): 505–509.
2. See Lin Xiang, '*Shudun kao*' (A study on the Shu shields), *Sichuan wenwu*, 1992, a special issue on Sanxingdui culture, pp. 18–25.

a

b

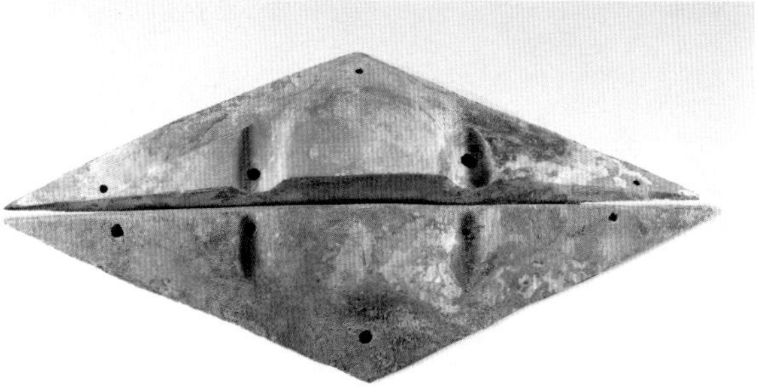

c

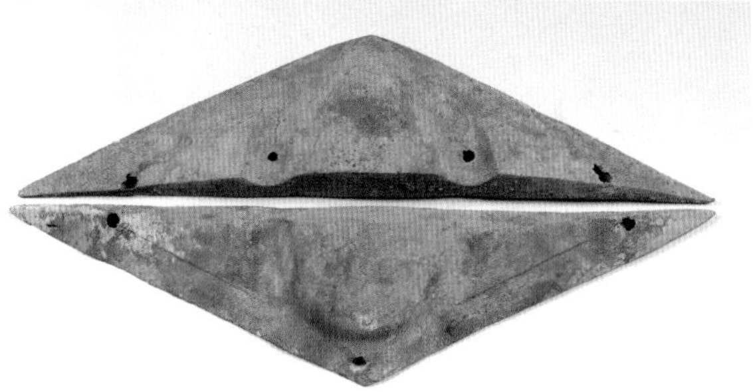

d

29 Diamond-shaped fittings
銅眼形器

Late Shang (c. 1200–1100 BCE)
Bronze
a: Single-part form (K2-3: 152),
length 54 cm, width 23.2 cm, weight 975 g
b: Single-part form (K2-2: 158-2),
length 57 cm, width 24 cm, weight 1050 g
c: Two-part form (K2-3: 8; K2-3: 197),
length 54.8 cm, width 25.6 cm, weight 902 g
d: Two-part form (K2-2: 176; K2-3: 105),
length 54.6 cm, width 26 cm, weight 950 g
Excavated from Sanxingdui Pit II
商代晚期
a. 長：54 cm寬：23.2 cm; b. 長：57 cm寬：24 cm
c. 長：54.8 cm寬：25.6 cm; d. 長：54.6 cm寬：26 cm

About seventy-one diamond-shaped fittings like these were discovered in Pit II. They are all thinly cast, hollow and fall into three types: a single-part form, two-part form and four-part form. The diamond shape and the raised circular centres led the archaeologists to speculate that they may indicate eyes. They were probably attached to the huge statues made in other materials or part of the buildings, for all of the pieces have small holes. In addition to the diamond-shaped fittings, Pit II also yielded a group of thirty-three fittings in the shape of bulbs or cylinders, which are very similar to the protruding eyes of the masks (cat. nos 15–16) in that they are also thinly cast, hollow and have holes for attachment. Like most of the round eyes of the animal masks (cat. nos 17–19), these fittings were painted in black with the double-circle motif on the bulging area of the cylinders. It is assumed such fittings might have represented pupils. Although we have no certain idea as to the precise function of these objects, their presence along with the dramatic protruding eyes and independent eye fittings, all in bronze, does suggest that the motif of the eye was of particular significance to the people of Sanxingdui.

a

b

30 Ceremonial dagger *ge*
銅戈

Late Shang (c. 1200–1100 BCE)
Bronze
a Height 19.2 cm, width 6.1 cm, weight 70 g
b Height 20.9 cm; width 5.8 cm; weight 73 g
Excavated from Sanxingdui Pit II (K2-3: 236; K2-3: 144-8)

商代晚期，a. 長：19.2 cm 寬：6.1 cm
b. 長：20.9 cm 寬：5.8 cm

Some sixty-one bronze *ge* daggers were excavated from the Sanxingdui pits (44 pieces from Pit I, 17 pieces from Pit II). Such *ge* daggers typically have short, pointed blades with serrated edges on both sides and a ridge in the centre. A hole in the upper part of the tang is perhaps intended to attach it to a handle. The *ge* daggers were essentially made as ritual rather than military weapons as evidenced by the blunt edges.

While the bronze vessels excavated in Sanxingdui pits are familiar Shang types, the bronze *ge* daggers represent one of the most characteristic Shu weapons.

When the Sanxingdui occupation ended mysteriously during the early Western Zhou, and the centre of Shu kingdom moved to the present-day Chengdu area, most of the typical bronze types which flourished at Sanxingdui died out. The *ge* dagger was one of the few types that endured. It was the principal bronze weapon of the Warring States period (476–221 BCE) in this area.

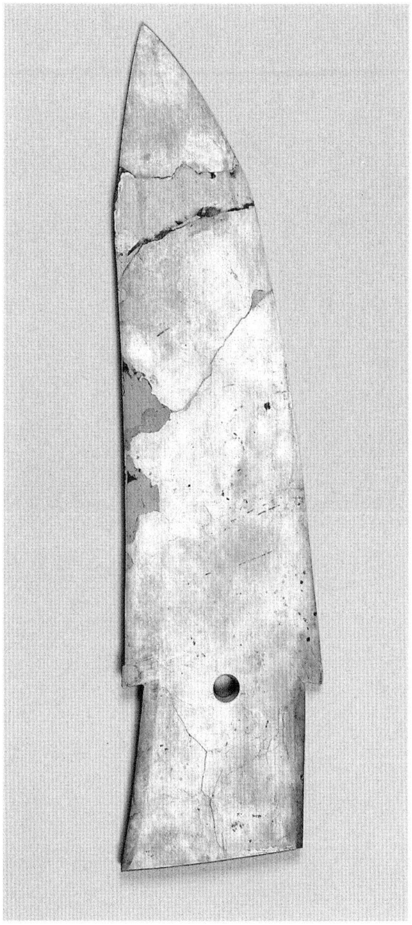

31 Ceremonial *ge* dagger
玉戈

Middle Shang dynasty (c. 1300 BCE)
Jade
Length 37 cm, width 8.35 cm, thickness 0.8 cm; weight 380 g; excavated from Sanxingdui Pit I (K1: 08)
商代中期， 長：37 cm 寬：8.35 cm

Although the bronzes are the most striking finds at Sanxingdui, the most numerous discoveries are works in jade. During the past half a century, over one thousand jades and some two thousand stone implements have been found at the Sanxingdui site. The majority of jades are in the form of discs, tools or ceremonial weapons. The range of types is confined to ritual jades, rather than personal ornaments or utilitarian objects.

Among 129 jades in various shapes found in Pit I, there were eighteen *ge* daggers; jade versions of their bronze counterparts. The shapes of jade *ge* current in the metropolitan Shang area were taken as the norm, as evidenced by the rich finds excavated from the tomb of Fuhao (tomb of a consort of the Shang King Wuding) at Anyang in Henan, which dates from the 13th century BCE.[1] Archaeologists have categorised the jade *ge* daggers into three types: this one, representative of type two, is made of an opaque, creamy yellow jade with a slightly curved blade, a ridge at the pointed end and a single hole in the tang.

1. Cf. Institute of Archaeology (1980), monochrome pls 107–113; colour pls 17–18.

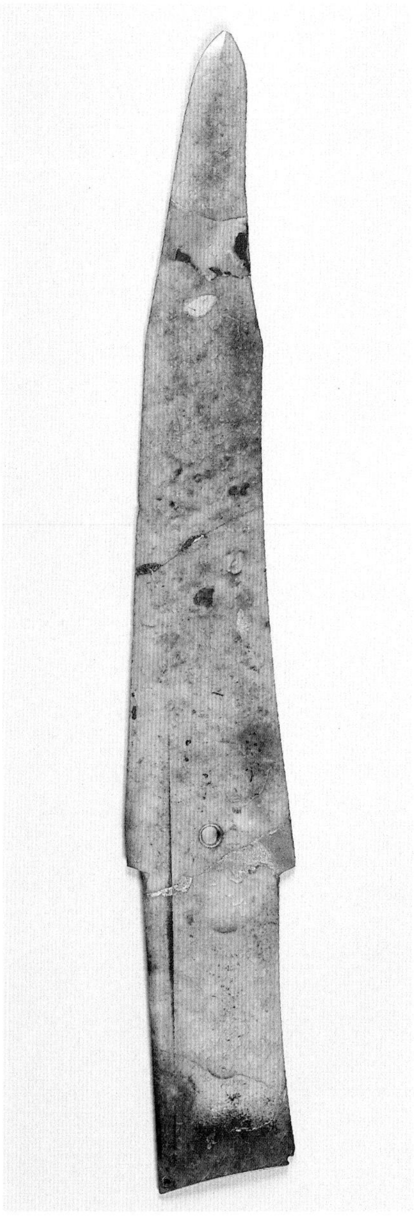

32 Ceremonial *ge* dagger

玉戈

Late Shang dynasty (c. 1200–1100 BCE)
Jade
Length 44.8 cm, width 5.5 cm, thickness 0.6 cm, weight 220 g; excavated from Sanxingdui Pit II (K2-3: 314-1)

商代晚期， 長：44.8 cm 寬：5.5 cm

This is one of the twenty-one jade *ge* daggers discovered from Pit II all of which were found neatly placed in the southeast corner. Unlike the bronze objects, the jade *ge* daggers were not deliberately broken before they were dumped in the pit. They were only affected by fire damage. This example, representative of type three, shows a different feature to previous entry. It has a long pointed blade with an extended tip that turns slightly at an angle to the main blade. The shallow ridge is evident only at the pointed end.

33 Ceremonial trapezoidal blade *zhang*

玉璋

Late Shang (c. 1200–1100 BCE)
Jade
Length 68.8 cm, width 7.5 cm, thickness 1 cm; weight 875 g, excavated from Sanxingdui Pit II (K2-3: 324)

商代晚期， 長：68.8 cm 寬：7.5 cm

Jade blades in this form are known by the later name '*zhang*'. So far, over two hundred blades of this type have been discovered over a wide range in China. The jade *zhang* emerged during the period of the Longshan culture (c. 2500–2000 BCE), flourished in the Xia and early Shang dynasties (c. 2100–1600 BCE), and declined during the late Shang to early Western Zhou period (c. 12th –10th centuries BCE). It has been defined as an important ritual object in Western Zhou ritual texts. Yet the best evidence that *zhang* was indeed used for ritual purposes is in the Sanxingdui finds. A tiny bronze figure of a kneeling man found in Pit II clearly holds a *zhang* (p. 32, fig. 6).

Evidence of its significance to the people of Sanxingdui is the fact that some fifty-seven jade *zhang* were discovered from the two pits (40 examples from Pit I, and 17 examples from Pit II). Although the jade *zhang* is a familiar Shang type, many variants found in Sanxingdui pits are eccentric in design, as this blade exemplifies. Dark green in colour, the piece has a sharpened and splayed end, as well as the hooks and small spikes on each side down close to the tang. The deep V-shaped end and the open work of hooks carved in spirals, reflect the regional peculiarities incorporated in the interpretation of the orthodox form of the *zhang* by Sanxingdui craftsmen. The enormous scale is one other unique feature of the Sanxingdui *zhang* blades. Pit I has yielded a large fragment of a jade *zhang* measuring 159.2 cm in length. The example illustrated here is probably one of the longest intact trapezoidal blades so far discovered in China.

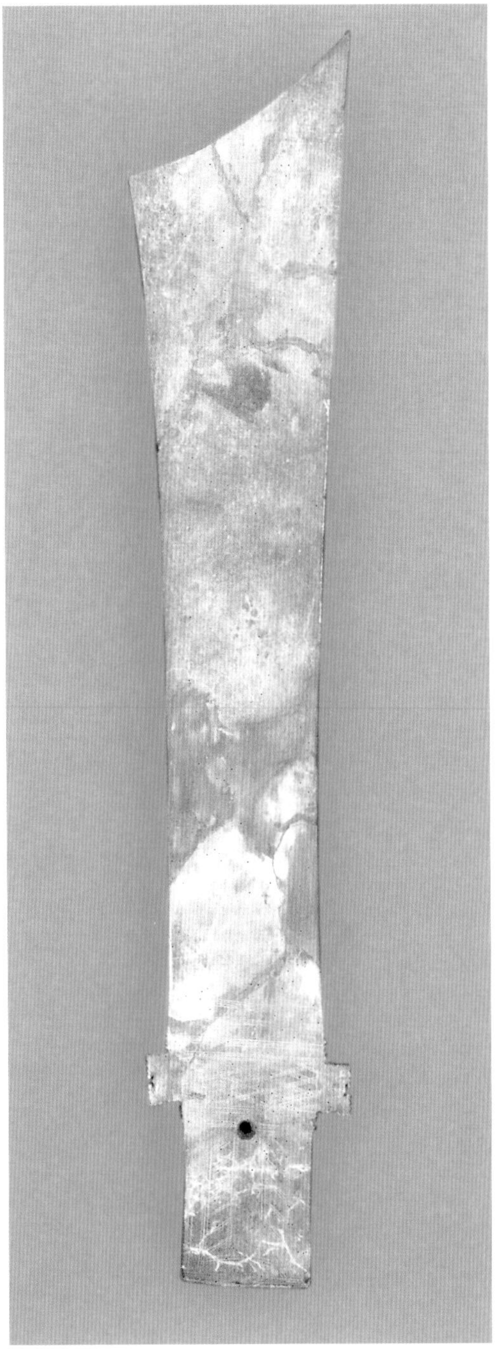

34 Ceremonial trapezoidal blade *zhang*
玉璋

Middle Shang (c. 1300 BCE),
Jade
Length 55.2 cm, width 9.6 cm, thickness 0.8 cm; weight 683 g; excavated in 1984 from Sanxingdui site (1984GS)
商代中期， 長：55.2 cm 寬：9.6 cm

The variety in form and style of the *zhang* blades discovered at the Sanxingdui site have led archaeologists to speculate that they were made in different periods of occupation. The early types with shallow, splayed ends and symmetrically arranged notches may have been first imported from northern China during the Erlitou period (21–17 centuries BCE) of the Xia dynasty. They continued to be made locally during the Shang dynasty with reference to more ancient pieces that had presumably been collected and handed down over generations. Over time, the forms were greatly elaborated with regional peculiarities. Besides its possible early date, this greyish jade *zhang* also shows an interesting feature common to many Shang ritual jades: the geometric patterns engraved on the hook and tang. This is the most popular decorative technique employed by the Sanxingdui craftsmen on jade objects.

35 Pendant *pei*
玉戚形佩

Middle Shang (c. 1300 BCE)
Jade
Length 12.4 cm, width 6.72 cm, thickness 1.65 cm; weight 183 g, excavated from Sanxingdui Pit I (K1: 235)
商代中期， 長：12.4 cm 寬：6.72 cm

While the group of objects in jade such as the *ge* daggers and *zhang* blades resemble closely those of the Shang culture in Henan and elsewhere, some objects are peculiar to Sanxingdui and not seen elsewhere. One such type is this jade pendant, known by the later term '*pei*'. The pendant is an almost oval shape with a pointed top. A small hole, which is off centre, is drilled from one side. Below the hole, there are four pairs of parallel lines incised across the centre to join notches on each side. The area between each pair of lines has been carved in relief.

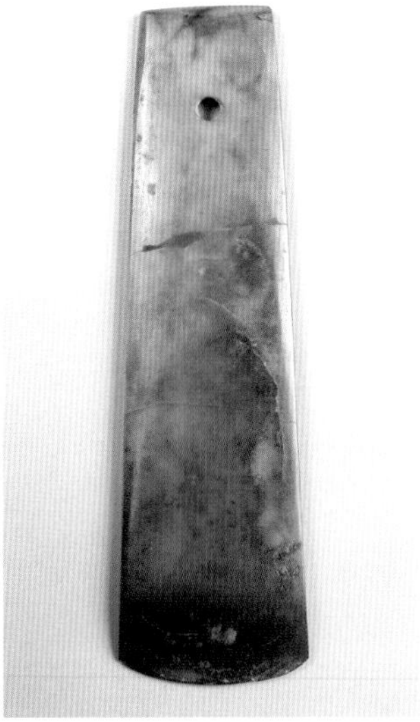

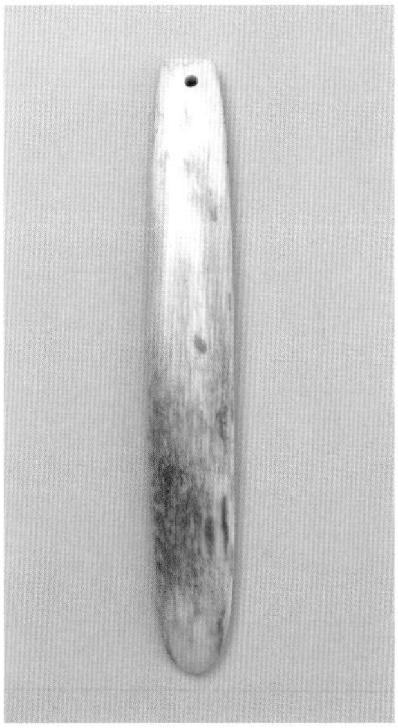

36 Ceremonial axe

玉斧

Late Shang (c. 1200–1100 BCE)
Jade
Height 20 cm, width 6 cm; weight 191 g; excavated from Sanxingdui Pit II (K2-3: 322-5)
商代晚期， 長：20 cm 寬：6 cm

The jade axe derives from the utilitarian tool used in stone age societies. Its adoption as a ritual object signifies its power in agriculture and in war. Ceremonial axes were found in a wide area of China. Sanxingdui Pit I yielded seventeen examples, yet only one was discovered in Pit II. This piece is in the form of a rectangular tablet, slightly flared towards the bottom. Except for the slightly round cutting edge, all sides of the tablet are strongly bevelled. The cutting edge was polished to a sharp edge on one side. There is a single hole drilled in the upper area.

37 Ceremonial chisel

玉鑿

Late Shang (c. 1200–1100 BCE)
Jade
Height 19.6 cm, width 2.9 cm, thickness 1.5 cm; weight 159 g; excavated from Sanxingdui Pit II (K2-2: 322-9)
商代晚期， 高：19.6 cm 寬：2.9 cm

The jade chisel is another example of a type of object which has never been found elsewhere. What archaeologists have termed 'chisel' is a thin, oblong object tapered toward one or both ends. Seventy-eight similar jade chisels were excavated from the Sanxingdui pits. Well polished and pierced at the top, this example is one of forty-three jade chisels found inside a bronze vessel *lei* (K2-2: 88) in Pit II. This may well provide a clue to their function: obviously they were jade copies of stone tools and made for ritual, rather than utilitarian purposes.

38 Ritual jade *cong*
玉琮

Shang (c. 1600–1100 BCE)
Jade
Height 7.23 cm, width 8.34 cm, inner perimeter 7 cm; weight 109 g; excavated in 1929 at Sanxingdui site (00909)
商代， 高：7.23 cm 寬：8.34 cm

A roughly square cross-section with a circular bore, the jade *cong* is one of the most familiar of jade ritual objects of ancient China. Although the Western Zhou ritual texts mentioned that the *cong* was an offering to the earth, its exact meaning and function in the culture of the Neolithic period to the Shang, as well as in the context of Sanxingdui, is still uncertain. The number of *cong* discovered throughout late Neolithic and Bronze age tombs and burials is testimony to its significance in ancient rituals and ceremonies.

However, in comparison with other forms in jade, the *cong* appears less favoured by Sanxingdui inhabitants, as only one example (K1: 11-2) was discovered from both pits. This *cong* belongs to a group of nearly four hundred ritual jades found accidentally in 1929 at the Sanxingdui site by a local farmer. It is decorated on its translucent green body with three groups of horizontal lines on its four corners. The two vertical lines on each side create an impression that cuts the outside cube into four separate sections abutting the inner cylinder.

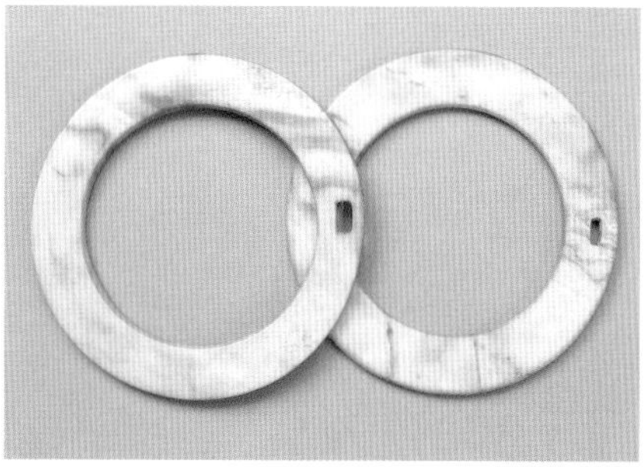

39 Ring *huan*
玉環

Shang (c. 1600–1100 BCE)
Jade
a. Diameter 9.28 cm, thickness 0.65 cm, weight 55 g
b. Diameter 9.21 cm; thickness 0.63 cm; weight 46 g
Excavated in 1987 at Sanxingdui site (87GSZJ: 10; 87GSZJ: 12)
商代， a. 直徑：9.28 cm; b. 直徑：9.21 cm

Discs and rings are the major forms of ancient ritual jade, existing as early as the fifth millennium BCE in China. The Western Zhou ritual texts defined the disc *bi* as an offering to the heaven. The term '*bi*' has been applied to the discs with proportionally small central holes. If the hole is larger in proportion to the area of the whole, then the jade is generally known as a *huan*. There were two types of rings made in Sanxingdui: the plain ring and the ring with a central vertical collar. Judging from the burials of the two pits, the collared ring was the favourite form. Besides a group of thirteen collared rings in jade, there were some fifty-eight bronze replicas. This pair of rings was excavated in 1987 at the Sanxingdui site, rather than from either of the pits. They show a rich opaque creamy yellow with brown and green veins. An unusual feature is the small rectangular hole drilled on the one side of the ring.

Sanxingdui Pit I

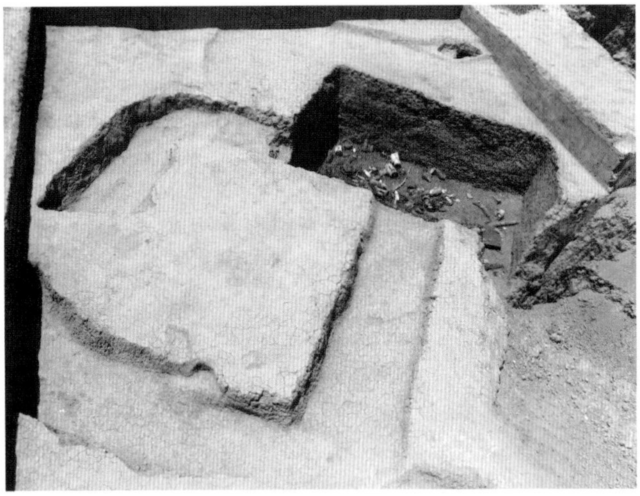

Sanxingdui Pit II

Selected Bibliography

Bagley, Robert W., 'Sacrificial Pits of the Shang Period at Sanxingdui in Guanghan County, Sichuan Province', *Arts Asiatiques*, vol. XLIII (1988): 78–86.

———, 'A Shang City in Sichuan Province', *Orientations*, November (1990): 52–67.

Chang, K.C., *Art, Myth and Ritual: The Path to Political Authority in Ancient China*, Cambridge: Harvard University Press, 1984.

Chen De'an, 'Sanxingdui jisikeng chutu qingtong mianju yanjiu (A Study on the Bronze Masks Excavated in the Sacrificial Pits at Sanxingdui)', *Sichuan wenwu*, 1992, a special issue on the Sanxingdui culture, pp. 38–44.

———, et al., *Sanxingdui: Changjiang shangyou wenming zhongxing tansuo* (Sanxingdui: A Study of the Centre of Culture in the Upper Yangzi River Region), Chengdu: Sichuan renmin Press, 1998.

Chen Xiandan, 'Guanghan Sanxingdui yizhi fajue gaikuang, chubu fenqi – jianlun 'zaoshu wenhua' de tezheng jiqi fazhan (A General Excavation Report and Preliminary Periodization of the Sanxingdui Site at Guanghan, with a Discussion of the Characteristics and Development of the Early Shu Culture)', *Nanfang minzu kaogu* (Southern Ethnology and Archaeology), 2 (1989): 213–231.

———, 'Guanghan Sanxingdui yi, erhao keng liangge wenti de tantao (A Discussion of the Questions Relating to the Pit I and Pit II Finds at Sanxingdui in Guanghan)', *Wenwu*, 5 (1989): 1–20

Childs-Johnson, Elizabeth, 'Shangren liyi yishu zhong de Shamanjiao tezheng ji dui Sichuan Guanghan Sanxingdui xin faxian de tuice (The Shamanistic Character in Shang Ritual and Speculation on the New Discoveries Made at Sanxingdui in Guanghan, Sichuan)', trans. by Shi Yingping, *Nanfang minzu kaogu*, 2 (1989): 65–68.

———, 'The Metamorphic Image: A Predominant Theme in the Ritual Art of Shang China', *The Museum Far Eastern Antiquities, Bulletin* no. 70 (1998): 5–172.

Dept. of Archaeology of Northwest University, 'Xi'an Laoniupo Shangdai mudi de fajue (The Excavation of the Shang Tombs at Laoniupo in Xi'an)', *Wenwu*, 6 (1988): 1–22.

Goepper, Roger, et al. *Das Alte China*. Kunsthaus Zurich, 1996.

Graham, D.C., 'Hanzhou fajue jianbao (A Preliminary Report of the Hanzhou Excavation)', *Journal of the West China Border Research*, vol. vi, 1933–34.

Hu Changyu and Cai Ge, 'Yufu kao (About Yufu)', *Sichuan wenwu*, 1992, a special issue on Sanxingdui culture, pp. 26–33.

Institute of Archaeology, *Yinxu fuhao mu* (The Fuhao Tomb at Yin Site), Beijing: Wenwu Press, 1980.

Institute of Archaeology of Sichuan Province, *Sanxingdui jisikeng* (Excavation of the Sacrificial Pits at Sanxingdui), Beijing: Wenwu Press, 1999.

Kesner, Ladislav, '*Taotie* Reconsidered: Remarks on Shang Theriomorphic Imagery', *Artibus Asiae*, vol. LI: 1/2 (1991), pp. 29–50.

Lee, Sherman E., et al., *China: 5000 Years*, New York: Guggenheim Museum, 1998.

Lévi-Strauss, Claude, *Totemism*, translated by Rodney Needham, London : Merlin Press, 1964.

Li Boqian, 'Chenggu qingtongqi yu zhaoqi Shu wenhua (The Chenggu Bronzes and the Early Shu Culture)', *Kaogu yu wenwu*, 2 (1983): 66–70.

Lin Xiang, 'Shujiu tanyuan – Ba, Shu de 'Shaman shi wenhua' yanjiu zhiyi (Origins of the Shu Wine – The Shamanistic Culture in Ba and Shu, part one)', *Nanfang minzu kaogu*, vol. 1 (1987): 73–86.

Li Shaoming, et al., ed., *Sanxingdui yu Bashu wenhua* (Sanxingdui and the Ba-Shu Culture), Chengdu: Bashu shushe Press, 1993.

Li Xueqing, *Zouchu yigu shidai* (From Doubt to Historical Certainty), Shenyang: Liaoning University Press, 1997.

Lommel, Andreas, *Masks: Their Meaning and Function*, trans. by Nadia Fowler, London: Paul Elek Books, 1972.

Luo Kaiyu, 'Sanxingdui yizhi yu gudai xi'nan wenhua guanxi chulun (A Preliminary Discussion of the Relationship between the Sanxingdui Site and the Culture of the Ancient Southwest Region)', *Sichuan wenwu*, 1989, a special issue on Sanxingdui Culture, pp. 31–36.

Meng Wentong, *Bashu gushi lunshu* (Discussions on the Ancient History of Ba and Shu), Chengdu: Sichuan renmin Press, 1981.

Metropolitan Museum of Art, *The Great Bronze Age of China*, New York, 1980.

Museum of Sichuan University and The Chengdu Municipal Museum, 'Chengdu Zhihuijie Zhoudai yizhi fajue baogao (Report on the Excavation of a Zhou Dynasty Site at Zhihuijie in Chengdu)', *Nanfang minzu kaogu*, 1 (1987): 171–210.

Rawson, Jessica., *Chinese Jade: From the Neolithic to the Qing*, London: British Musem Press, 1995

———. et al. *Mysteries of Ancient China*, London: British Museum Press, 1996.

Ren Naiqiang, *Sichuan shanggushi xintan* (A New Investigation of the Ancient History of Sichuan), Chengdu: Sichuan renming Press, 1986.

Sichuan Provincial Administration for Cultral Relics, et al., 'Guanghan Sanxingdui yizhi (The Sanxingdui Site at Guanghan)', *Kaogu xuebao*, 2 (1987): 227–254.

———, 'Guanghan Sanxingdui yizhi yihao jisikeng fajue jianbao (A Brief Report on the Excavation of the Sacrificial Pit I at Sanxingdui Site in Guanghan)', *Wenwu*, 10 (1987): 1–15.

———, 'Chengdu shi'erqiao shangdai jianzhu yizhi diyiqi fajue jianbao (A Brief Report on the Excavation of the Shang Site at Shi'erqiao in Chengdu)', *Wenwu*, 12 (1987): 1–23.

———, 'Guanghan Sanxingdui yizhi er'hao jisikeng fajue jianbao (A Brief Report on the Excavation of the Sacrificial Pit II at Sanxingdui Site in Guanghan)', *Wenwu*, 5 (1989): 1–20.

Song Zhimin, 'Zaoqi Shu wenhua de zai tantao (A Further Discussion of the Early Shu Culture)', *Chengdu wenwu*, 1 (1989): 1-9; 2 (1989): 11–14.

Sun Hua, 'Tujing tongmianxiang – shuren de zunshen zhulong he Cancong (Masks with Protruding Eyes – the Venerated Deities of Shu People: Zhulong and Cancong)', *Post of the Chinese Cultural Relics*, 24 May 1992.

———, 'Guanyu Sanxingdui qiwukeng ruogan wenti de bianzheng (Discussion of Questions of Storage Pits in Sanxingdui)' *Sichuan Wenwu*, 4 (1993): 3–11; 5 (1993): 5–7.

Tang Jinyu et al., 'Shaanxi sheng Chenggu xian chutu Yin-Shang tongqi zhengli baogao (A Report on the Excavation of Bronzes of the Shang Dynasty at Chenggu County in Shaanxi Province)', *Kaogu*, 3 (1980): 211–218.

Wu, Hung, 'All about the Eyes: Two Groups of Sculptures from the Sanxingdui Culture.' *Orientations*, September (1997): 58–66.

Xu Chaolong, 'Sanxingdui 'Jisikeng shuo' changyi – Jiantan Yufu he Duyu zhi guanxi (A Contradictory View on the So-called 'Sacrificial pits', and an Appraisal of the Relationship between Yufu and Duyu)', *Sichuan wenwu*, 5 (1992): 32–38; 6 (1992): 40–47.

———, ''Qushang' zaikao (A Further Investigation on 'Qushang')', in Li Shaoming, et al., 1993, pp. 275–284.

Yu Xingwu, *Jiagu wenzi shilin* (Interpretations of the Oracle Writings), Beijing: Zhonghua Press, 1983.

Zhao Dianzeng, 'Sanxingdui kaogu faxian yu Bashushi yanjiu (The Archaeological Discoveries at Sanxingdui and the Studies of Ba-Shu history)', *Sichuan wenwu*, 1992, a special issue on Sanxingdui culture, pp. 3–12.

———, 'The Sacrificial Pits at Sanxingdui', in Roger Goepper (1996), pp. 129, and Jessica Rawson (1996), pp. 232–239.